FamilyCircle

Desserts

AND AFTER-DINNER TREATS

The Family Circle® Promise of Success

Welcome to the world of Confident Cooking,
created for you in the **Family Circle® Test Kitchen**,
where recipes are double-tested by
our team of home economists to achieve a
high standard of success – and delicious
results every time.

MURDOCH BOOKS®

Sydney • London • Vancouver • New York

C O N T E

Apple Pie, page 28

Chilled Lime Soufflé, page 41

Peach Charlotte with Melba Sauce, page 27

Mixed Fruit and Nut Balls, page 84

Paris Brest, page 66

The test kitchen, where our recipes are double-tested by our team of home economists to achieve a high standard of success and delicious results every time.

When we test our recipes, we rate them for ease of preparation. The following cookery ratings are on the recipes in this book, making them easy to use and understand.

The Publisher thanks the following for their assistance in the photography for this book: Wedgwood; Royal Doulton; The Bay Tree; The Melbourne Shop; Pacific East India Co; Home & Garden, Skygarden.

Macerated Fruits with Mascarpone, page 80

A single Cooking with Confidence symbol indicates a recipe that is simple and generally quick to make – perfect for beginners.

Two symbols indicate the need for just a little more care and a little more time.

Three symbols indicate special dishes that need more investment in time, care and patience—but the results are worth it.

Front cover, clockwise from top left: Lemon Meringue Pie (p. 64), Mango Mille Feuille (p. 47), Crème Caramel (p. 78), Chocolate Clusters (p. 91), Chocolate Praline Triangles (p. 94) and Caramel Squares (page 103). Inside front cover: Spicy Cheesecake (p. 63). Back cover: Cappuccino Brownies (p 30).

Mixed Nut Biscotti and Choc-dipped Macaroons, page 98

Praline Ice-cream with Toffee Glass, page 9

Sweet Sensations

A great dessert can be the crowning glory of a great meal, whether you're entertaining or simply sharing good food with the family. Desserts offer a wonderful opportunity to express your creativity, and even the simplest dish can be impressive. There is something very special, festive—sometimes even forbidden—about these sweet treats, and even more so about the delectable morsels you can make at home to offer with coffee and liqueurs.

It's important to use only the best quality ingredients in desserts, especially fresh fruits in season, to ensure the best colour, texture and flavour. This is also an opportunity to indulge yourself or your guests with richer or more exotic ingredients than you would use every day.

Many of the recipes in this book feature one of the following as an ingredient or accompaniment:

Crème fraîche: A mix of fresh and sour cream. The added bacterial culture sours the flavour and gives it a particularly rich texture. Crème fraîche is used in both sweet and savoury dishes, and is great with pies and fresh fruits.

Thickened cream: Pouring cream to which gelatine has been added. It is good for whipping and keeps well.

Thick pure cream: Cream with a higher fat content than pouring cream or thickened cream. It makes a rich dessert accompaniment or topping and requires no whipping—just spoon it on in dollops. There are many brands on the market nowadays.

Mascarpone: A rich, high-fat, soft creamy cheese which originated in Italy. Resembling thick cream it has a sweetish, slightly tart flavour and is delicious with fruit.

Preparing a soufflé dish

To achieve an attractive height on hot soufflés and contain the mixture, a paper collar is fastened around the dish. Allow enough room in the oven for rising. Soufflés should be served immediately on removal from the oven as they start to sink rapidly in cold air.

Chilled soufflés have a foil collar fastened around the dish to hold the mixture until it is set and to create the illusion of a risen souffle.

For chilled soufflés, wrap foil strips around dishes; secure with string.

Carefully remove the foil collar when soufflé is set, before serving.

USING GELATINE

Gelatine is a setting agent used in a range of sweet and savoury dishes. It is almost tasteless so does not alter the flavour, but is essential in certain chilled moulds and creams, enabling them to set and hold their shape.

Gelatine is commercially available as powder (in sachets), or small leaves. Powder is the easiest to use. One sachet of powdered gelatine contains three teaspoons and is the equivalent of six gelatine leaves.

When using gelatine, the temperature of the setting liquid and the amount of gelatine used is critical. The more that is used, the firmer the result. (Note: Not all ingredients can

Sprinkle gelatine powder onto cold water in a small bowl.

Stir the solution with a fork to dissolve the gelatine.

If using leaf gelatine, squeeze out water after softening.

be used with gelatine. Some fruits—for example pineapple—contain an enzyme which will prevent it setting.)

Gelatine should first be softened in cold water; warm or hot water will cause it to clump together. Sprinkle powdered gelatine over the water in a small bowl and place in a larger bowl of hot water until the gelatine softens. Stir with a fork to dissolve it.

Leaf gelatine should be softened in a bowl by first covering with cold water. Soak for 5 minutes or until the gelatine is very soft. Lift it out in your hand, squeeze out the water and place softened gelatine leaf in a small bowl over a pan of simmering water. Shake pan gently until gelatine has melted; do not stir. Lift out a spoonful of liquid to check if the gelatine has melted completely.

The most important thing to remember when using gelatine is that the gelatine solution and the mixture to which it is added must be the same temperature or the gelatine will clump together. Stir the mixture well to distribute the gelatine evenly. Set in the refrigerator, not the freezer (too rapid chilling may cause the gelatine to crystallise and separate).

EQUIPMENT
These recipes use equipment that is standard in most kitchens nowadays: a range of tins and baking dishes, electric beaters (hand-held is just as good), the food processor.

A baba tin or mould is a bucket shape and is used for baking rum babas. A dariole mould is similar. Moulds and ramekin dishes for soufflés and other puddings can be found in department stores or specialist kitchenware stores.

Presentation is important with desserts and sweets. For maximum impact, serve in attractive or unusual individual bowls and goblets, or on pretty serving dishes.

THINGS TO DO AHEAD
Nobody wants to disappear into the kitchen to slave over dessert at the end of a meal. Fortunately, even some of the most spectacular dishes in this book can be at least partially prepared ahead of time—a few hours or the day before. Many can also be served either hot or cold.

Using chocolate

Chocolate is one of the most popular dessert finishing touches, as well as a superb ingredient in many recipes. Handling it is quite easy, although it needs a little care. Chocolate decorations can be simple to make and look wonderful. **Note:** Cooking chocolate has the best flavour. Compound chocolate does not taste as good, but is great for decorating as it sets quickly.

Shavings and curls: Use a sharp knife or vegetable peeler to shave a block of chocolate along the edge to make long or short curls or shavings. Have chocolate at room temperature but not too soft. For large curls, melt chocolate and spread on a benchtop. Cool until almost set. Drag a large flat-bladed knife, held horizontally, towards you, applying constant downward pressure. Varying the pressure will determine the thickness of the curls. For very fat curls, use a metal ice-cream scoop. Fine gratings can be made with a vegetable grater.

Melted chocolate: This can be piped or drizzled on top of a dish in decorative patterns. Or pipe patterns onto a sheet of baking paper, allow to set and lift off carefully. Melted chocolate can also be used to make chocolate leaves or other shapes.

Melt chocolate in a bowl over simmering water or in a microwave.

1 Hot water method
Chop chocolate into even pieces; this helps it to melt uniformly. Place in a small heatproof bowl. Place bowl over a pan of gently simmering—not boiling—water and stir gently until chocolate melts. Be careful not to allow even a tiny amount of water or steam to come into contact with the chocolate (make sure the bowl or spoon is not wet) or it will immediately stiffen and turn into a rough, unworkable mass. Cool the chocolate slightly before using it, but use quickly before it sets.

2 Microwave method
To melt chocolate in the microwave, place chopped chocolate in a microwave-safe bowl. Microwave, uncovered, on High for 30 seconds. The timing will vary depending on the amount and type of chocolate and the wattage of the microwave. Test chocolate between bursts by stirring—it will hold its shape even when the inside is melted. If the outside melts, the chocolate on the inside will be burned.

To maintain the gloss of melted chocolate coatings it is better to prepare close to serving time and store in a cool place, rather than in the refrigerator. Tiny drops of moisture can form in the refrigerator and dull the surface.

Stir chocolate gently in a heatproof bowl over simmering water.

Stir microwaved chocolate to test whether the inside is melted.

Follow the storage time notes at the end of each recipe and do as much as possible ahead. Pastry cases can be baked and meringue cooked and re-crisped in a slow oven later. Refrigerated or frozen desserts need to be made well ahead, and some need time for flavours to develop. Decorate and garnish at the last minute. This will allow you to relax and enjoy creating, presenting—and eating—your desserts and after-dinner treats.

DESSERTS

Desserts can range from light and fruity to rich and creamy—there's one to suit every menu and occasion. When choosing a dessert, read the recipes through completely to get a sense of how much time the dish will take to prepare, as well as what ingredients you may need to buy. Also bear in mind how well the dessert's flavour and texture will marry with other courses you are planning to serve. Aim for balance, serving a lighter dessert after a heavy main course, and perhaps something memorably luscious to finish a lighter meal.

BLUEBERRY CREME BRULEE

Preparation time: 15 minutes + 3 hours refrigeration
Total cooking time: 15 minutes
Serves 6

250 g blueberries
1¼ cups cream
1¼ cups thick pure cream
1 vanilla pod
5 egg yolks
2 tablespoons caster sugar
¼ cup caster sugar, extra

➤ DIVIDE THE BLUEBERRIES between six ³/₄-cup capacity ramekin dishes.

1 Place the cream and thick pure cream in a medium pan and stir to combine. Split the vanilla pod lengthways and add it to the cream mixture. Place the pan over low heat and bring the mixture slowly to the boil. Combine the egg yolks and the sugar in a medium mixing bowl and, using a wire whisk, beat for 1 minute until mixture is pale and thickened slightly.

2 Pour the just-boiled cream mixture into the yolk mixture, whisking continuously, then discard the vanilla bean. Return the mixture to the pan and place the pan over low heat. Cook for about 5 minutes, stirring constantly, until the custard thickens—do not allow it to boil. Pour the custard over the blueberries in the ramekin dishes. Cool slightly, then refrigerate the dishes for at least 3 hours, until the custard mixture has set.

3 Preheat the grill until very hot. Sprinkle the extra caster sugar evenly onto the surface of each custard. Place the dishes under the grill and cook until the sugar on top has dissolved and caramelised. Remove the dishes from the heat and cool them completely before serving. (Do not place them in the refrigerator or the sugar will liquefy.) Serve Crème Brulées with extra fresh blueberries, if desired.

COOK'S FILE

Storage time: Crème Brûlées may be made and refrigerated up to a day before being served. Serve them within 30 minutes of caramelising the sugar. It is important that the brûlées are not refrigerated after this step.

Note: It is very important that the sugar topping of a crème brulée is caramelised quickly under very high heat. Keeping the brûlée under the grill for too long may cause the custard to bubble underneath. Place the brûlée as close as possible to the heat source and grill for about 3 minutes only.

Hint: Restaurants use an extremely hot commercial grill called a salamander, or a special brûlée iron (something like a branding iron), to achieve a hard toffee topping on this dessert. It is difficult to recreate this at home. However, good results can be had by melting the sugar with a small butane blowtorch, available from hardware stores. Follow the manufacturer's directions for use and be extremely careful if you decide to try this.

Variation: Raspberries, blackberries or small, very ripe strawberries can be used instead of the blueberries, if desired.

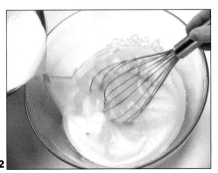

ALMOND ORANGE SYRUP PUDDING

Preparation time: 45 minutes
Total cooking time: 50 minutes
Serves 6–8

125 g butter
3/4 cup caster sugar
2 eggs, lightly beaten
3 teaspoons finely grated orange
    rind
1 1/2 cups ground almonds
1 cup semolina
1/4 cup orange juice

Syrup
1 cup orange juice, strained
1/2 cup caster sugar

Decoration
250 g punnet blueberries
icing sugar
thick pure cream

➤ PREHEAT OVEN to moderate 180°C. Brush a 20 cm ring tin with oil or melted butter; line the base with baking paper.

1 Using electric beaters, beat butter and sugar in a small bowl until light and creamy. Add eggs gradually, beating well between each addition. Add rind; beat until combined.

2 Transfer to a large bowl. Using a metal spoon, fold in almonds and semolina alternately with juice. Stir until ingredients are just combined and mixture is smooth. Spoon into prepared tin; smooth surface. Bake for 40 minutes, until skewer comes out clean when inserted into centre.

3 To make Syrup: Combine juice and sugar in small pan. Stir over medium heat until sugar completely dissolves. Bring to boil, reduce heat slightly and simmer 10 minutes. Remove from heat and cool slightly.

4 Brush half the warm syrup over warm cake while still in tin. Leave for 3 minutes, then place cake onto serving plate. Brush remaining syrup over surface of cake; cool. Fill centre of cake with blueberries dusted with icing sugar. Serve with cream.

COOK'S FILE

Storage time: Store pudding for up to 1 day in the refrigerator.

PRALINE ICE-CREAM WITH TOFFEE GLASS

Preparation time: 25 minutes + 6 hours refrigeration
Total cooking time: 7 minutes
Serves 4

70 g almonds (with skins)
1/4 cup caster sugar
3/4 cup cream
250 g mascarpone
125 g white chocolate, melted and cooled
2 tablespoons sugar

➤ LINE A flat baking tray with foil; brush foil lightly with oil.

1 Combine almonds and sugar in a small pan over low heat. Tilt pan slightly (do not stir) and watch until sugar melts and turns golden—this should take about 3–5 minutes.

2 Pour mixture onto prepared tray, leave until set and completely cold. Break into chunks, place into a plastic bag and crush with a rolling pin, or process briefly in a food processor until crumbly in texture.

3 Whip cream until stiff peaks form. Place mascarpone and chocolate in a large mixing bowl; stir to combine. Using a metal spoon, fold in whipped cream and crushed praline. Transfer to a 4-cup capacity ceramic or glass bowl, freeze for 6 hours or overnight. Remove from freezer 15 minutes before serving to soften slightly. Serve scoops of ice-cream decorated with Toffee Glass. Serve with fresh figs and dessert wafers, if desired

4 To make Toffee Glass: Line a flat baking tray with aluminium foil, brush lightly with oil. Sprinkle sugar evenly onto prepared tray. Place under hot grill for 2 minutes until sugar is melted and golden. Check

often towards the end of cooking time as sugar may burn quickly. Remove from heat, leave until set and completely cold, then break into shards.

COOK'S FILE

Storage time: Praline Ice-cream may be made up to 2 days in advance; cover tightly in the freezer. Toffee glass is best made within 30 minutes of serving, particularly if the weather is humid.

STICKY DATE PUDDING

Preparation time: 30 minutes
Total cooking time: 55 minutes
Serves 6–8

200 g dates, pitted and chopped
1 cup water
1 teaspoon bicarbonate of soda
100 g butter
2/3 cup caster sugar
2 eggs, lightly beaten
1 teaspoon vanilla essence
1 1/2 cups self-raising flour

Sauce
1 cup soft brown sugar
1/2 cup cream
100 g butter

➤ PREHEAT OVEN to moderate 180°C. Brush a 20 cm square cake tin with oil or melted butter. Line base with baking paper.

1 Combine dates and water in a small pan. Bring to the boil; remove from heat. Stir in soda and set aside to cool to room temperature.

2 Using electric beaters, beat butter and sugar in a small bowl until light and creamy. Add eggs gradually, beating thoroughly after each addition. Add essence, beat until combined. Transfer to a large bowl.

3 Using a metal spoon, fold in flour and dates with liquid and stir until just combined—do not over-beat. Pour into prepared tin, bake for 50 minutes, until a skewer comes out clean when inserted into centre of pudding. Leave in tin for 10 minutes before turning out and cutting into serving pieces.

4 To make Sauce: Combine sugar, cream and butter in a small pan; stir until butter melts and sugar dissolves. Bring to boil, reduce heat and simmer 2 minutes. Cut pudding into wedges, place on serving plates. Pour hot sauce over. Serve immediately, with cream and raspberries, if desired.

COOK'S FILE

Storage time: Pudding can be made up to 8 hours in advance. Cool and store in an airtight container. Sauce may be made up to 2 hours in advance; reheat to serve. Pudding need not be reheated—just cover each piece with the hot sauce.

DOUGHNUT BALLS WITH STRAWBERRY SAUCE

Preparation time: 10 minutes
Total cooking time: 10 minutes
Serves 4–6

2 eggs
2 tablespoons oil
2 tablespoons water
¹/3 cup caster sugar

1³/4 cups self-raising flour
oil for frying
³/4 cup caster sugar

Strawberry Sauce
**300 g fresh or thawed frozen
strawberries**
¹/2 cup strawberry jam

1 WHISK EGGS, oil, water and sugar until smooth. Stir in sifted flour, mix to a soft dough. Roll 2 teaspoons of mixture into balls with floured hands. Repeat with remaining mixture.

2 Heat oil in large pan to moderately hot. Deep-fry balls until cooked through and lightly browned. Roll in sugar to coat. Serve hot with Sauce, ice-cream and strawberries, if desired.

3 To make Sauce: Process strawberries and jam until smooth.

COOK'S FILE

Storage time: Serve immediately.

GINGER PUMPKIN PUDDING WITH BRANDY CUSTARD

Preparation time: 30 minutes
Total cooking time: 1 hour 35 minutes
Serves 6–8

125 g butter
3/4 cup brown sugar
2 eggs
3/4 cup cooked, mashed pumpkin
    (250 g raw, peeled)
2 cups self-raising flour
3 teaspoons ground ginger
1/2 teaspoon nutmeg
1/4 cup buttermilk

Brandy Custard
3 egg yolks
1/2 cup caster sugar
1 tablespoon custard powder
1 cup milk
1 cup cream
2 tablespoons brandy

➤ BRUSH AN 8-cup capacity pudding basin with oil or melted butter; line base with paper, grease paper.

1 Brush a large sheet of aluminium foil with oil or melted butter. Lay a sheet of baking paper over the greased side of the foil. Pleat them along the centre.

2 Using electric beaters, beat the butter and sugar in a small bowl until light and creamy. Add the eggs gradually, beating well after each addition. Add the mashed pumpkin and beat well. Transfer the mixture to a large mixing bowl.

3 Using a metal spoon, fold in the sifted flour, ginger and nutmeg alternately with the buttermilk. Stir until all ingredients are just combined and the mixture is almost smooth. Spoon mixture into the prepared basin, smooth the surface. Cover with the greased foil and paper, with foil side on top.

4 Place pudding basin lid over foil and secure clips. If you have no lid, lay a pleated tea towel over the foil, tie securely with string under lip of basin and knot four corners of tea towel together. It can then be used as a handle to lower the basin into the pan.

5 Place the basin on a trivet or upturned saucer in a large, deep pan. Carefully pour boiling water down the side of the pan to come halfway up the side of the basin. Bring to the boil, cover and cook for 1 hour 30 minutes. Do not allow the pan to boil dry—replenish with boiling water as necessary. When the pudding is cooked, leave it in the basin for 5 minutes before uncovering and inverting onto a plate. Serve with Brandy Custard. Decorate with glacé fruits, if desired.

6 To make Brandy Custard: Whisk egg yolks, sugar and custard powder together in a medium bowl. Combine milk and cream in a medium pan and bring just to the boil. Add gradually to the egg mixture, whisking continuously. Return mixture to the pan and stir over low heat for 5 minutes, until it thickens; do not boil. Stir in the brandy.

COOK'S FILE

Storage time: Ginger Pumpkin Pudding may be made up to 4 hours in advance. Serve it at room temperature, or reheat, covered with foil, in a moderate oven. Brandy Custard is best made close to serving time.

Note: Any kind of pumpkin can be used to make this pudding. Butternut pumpkin, although easier to handle, will give a blander flavour and paler colour than thicker-skinned varieties. To ensure a smooth texture, make sure the pumpkin is well cooked before mashing.

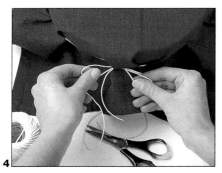

4

5

6

SUMMER BERRY TART

Preparation time: 35 minutes +
  20 minutes refrigeration
Total cooking time: 35 minutes
Serves 4–6

1 cup plain flour
90 g butter
2 tablespoons icing sugar
1–2 tablespoons water

Filling
3 egg yolks
2 tablespoons caster sugar
2 tablespoons cornflour
1 cup milk
1 teaspoon vanilla essence
250 g strawberries, halved
125 g blueberries

125 g raspberries
1–2 tablespoons baby apple gel

➤ PREHEAT OVEN to moderate
180°C. Process flour, butter and icing
sugar in food processor, using pulse
action, for 15 seconds or until fine and
crumbly. Add almost all the water,
process 20 seconds or until mixture
comes together; add more water if
necessary. Turn onto lightly floured
surface, press together until smooth.
1 Roll pastry to fit 20 cm round fluted
flan tin. Line tin with pastry, trim
edges; refrigerate 20 minutes. Cut a
sheet of greaseproof paper to cover
pastry-lined tin. Spread layer of dried
beans or rice evenly over paper. Bake
15 minutes. Remove from oven, discard paper and rice. Return to oven
for 15 minutes, or until lightly golden.

2 To make Filling: Place egg yolks,
sugar and cornflour in bowl, whisk
until pale. Heat milk in small pan until
almost boiling; remove from heat. Add
milk gradually to egg mixture, beating constantly. Strain into pan. Stir
constantly over low heat 3 minutes or
until it boils and thickens. Remove
from heat, add essence. Transfer to
bowl, cover with plastic wrap; cool.
3 Spread filling in cooled pastry shell.
Top with strawberries, blueberries
and raspberries. Place apple gel in a
pan of simmering water, or in the
microwave, until it liquefies. Brush gel
over fruit with a pastry brush.

COOK'S FILE

Storage time: Cook pastry up to a
day ahead. Store in airtight container.
Fill up to 4 hours before serving.

1

2

3

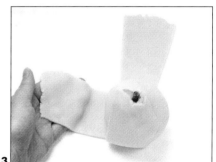

PEAR DUMPLINGS

Preparation time: 40 minutes + cooling
Total cooking time: 40 minutes
Serves 4

6 cups water
1 cup caster sugar
2 cinnamon sticks
2 cloves
4 medium pears
2 cups plain flour
150 g butter
2/3 cup icing sugar
1/3 cup lemon juice
1 egg, lightly beaten

➤ COMBINE WATER and sugar in a large pan. Stir over medium heat until sugar has completely dissolved. Add cinnamon and cloves, bring to boil.
1 Peel pears, leaving stems intact. Add to pan, cover and simmer gently for about 10 minutes, until just tender when tested with the point of a sharp knife. Carefully remove pears from pan, drain and cool completely.
2 Place flour and butter in a food processor; add icing sugar. Using pulse action, press button for 15 seconds or until mixture is fine and crumbly. Add almost all juice, process briefly until mixture comes together, adding more juice if necessary.
3 Preheat oven to moderate 180°C; line a flat baking tray with baking paper. Divide dough into 4 equal portions. Roll one portion out to a circle about 24 cm in diameter. Place a pear in centre of pastry, cut pastry into a wide cross; set cut-out sections aside. Carefully fold one section of pastry at a time up sides of pear, trimming and pressing edges together to neatly cover. Repeat with remaining pears.
4 Cut leaf shapes from leftover pastry. Brush pears all over with egg and attach leaves; brush leaves with egg. Place pears on prepared tray and bake for 30 minutes, until golden brown. Serve warm with custard and fresh fruit, if desired.

C O O K ' S   F I L E

Storage time: Pears may be poached up to 8 hours in advance. Assemble up to 4 hours in advance; cover with plastic wrap and refrigerate, ready to bake, until required.

CARAMEL BREAD PUDDING

Preparation time: 40 minutes +
overnight refrigeration
Total cooking time: 1 hour
Serves 6–8

2/3 cup caster sugar
2 tablespoons water
500 g panettone or brioche
1/2 cup caster sugar, extra
2 cups milk
2 wide strips lemon rind, white
pith removed
3 eggs, lightly beaten

➤ PREHEAT OVEN to moderate 180°C. Brush a 23 x 13 x 7 cm (5-cup capacity) loaf tin with oil or melted butter.

1 Combine sugar and water in a small pan; stir over medium heat without boiling until sugar has completely dissolved. Bring to the boil, reduce heat slightly and simmer without stirring for about 10 minutes, until syrup becomes a rich golden colour. Watch carefully towards the end of cooking to prevent burning. Pour into prepared tin; leave to cool.

2 Using a large serrated knife, cut panettone into 2 cm-thick slices and remove crusts. Trim into large pieces to fit tin in three layers, filling any gaps with panettone cut to size.

3 Combine extra sugar, milk and lemon rind in a medium pan. Stir over low heat until sugar has dissolved. Bring just to the boil, remove from heat and transfer mixture to a jug to cool and absorb lemon flavour. Remove rind, whisk in eggs. Pour milk mixture gradually into tin, allowing it to soak into panettone between each addition.

4 Place tin into a large baking dish and pour in enough hot water to come halfway up the sides. Bake for 50 minutes, until just set. Remove tin from baking dish and cool, then refrigerate pudding overnight. Turn onto a plate and cut into slices. Serve with fresh cream and fruit, if desired.

COOK'S FILE

Storage time: Caramel Bread Pudding can be stored for up to two days in the refrigerator.

PASSIONFRUIT TART

Preparation time: 30 minutes +
  20 minutes refrigeration
Total cooking time: 45 minutes
Serves 6–8

1 cup plain flour
¼ cup ground almonds
¼ cup caster sugar
60 g butter, chopped
2–3 tablespoons iced water

Filling
6 egg yolks
½ cup caster sugar
¾ cup fresh passionfruit
   pulp
75 g butter
1 teaspoon gelatine
1 tablespoon water
½ cup cream, whipped
1 cup cream, whipped, extra

➤ PREHEAT OVEN to moderate 180°C.

1 Place flour, almonds, sugar and butter in food processor. Press pulse button 30 seconds or until mixture is fine and crumbly. Add almost all water, process another 30 seconds or until mixture comes together (add more water if necessary). Press together on lightly floured surface until smooth.

2 Roll pastry to fit 23 cm fluted flan tin. Line tin with pastry, trim edges; refrigerate 20 minutes. Cut a sheet of greaseproof paper to cover pastry. Spread dried beans or rice evenly over paper. Bake 15 minutes. Remove from oven, discard paper and rice. Return to oven for another 15 minutes, or until pastry is lightly golden. Remove from oven and cool completely. Place yolks and sugar in a medium heatproof bowl. Whisk for 1 minute or until slightly thickened and pale. Add passionfruit pulp, stir to combine.

Stand bowl over a pan of simmering water, stir gently but constantly for 15 minutes, adding butter gradually, until mixture thickens. Remove from heat and cool slightly.

3 Combine gelatine with water in a small bowl. Stand bowl in hot water; stir until dissolved. Add gelatine mixture to passionfruit mixture, stir to combine thoroughly. Cool to room temperature, stirring occasionally. Fold in whipped cream. Spread cooled passionfruit mixture into pastry shell; smooth surface. Pipe extra whipped cream around edge of tart. Decorate with passionfruit pulp and mandarin segments, if desired. Refrigerate until required.

COOK'S FILE

Storage time: Pastry shell may be cooked up to a day in advance; cool and store in an airtight container until ready to fill.

WHITE CHOCOLATE CITRUS GATEAU

Preparation time: 1 hour
Total cooking time: 30 minutes
Serves 8–10

1 cup plain flour
4 eggs
2/3 cup caster sugar
60 g butter, melted and cooled

Filling
2 tablespoons cornflour
1/3 cup water
1/3 cup lemon juice
1/3 cup orange juice
1 teaspoon finely grated lemon rind
1 teaspoon finely grated orange rind
1/3 cup caster sugar
2 egg yolks
20 g butter

Topping
100 g white chocolate, chopped
1 cup cream

Decoration
1 large lemon
1 cup water
1/2 cup caster sugar
200 g white chocolate melts, melted

➤ PREHEAT OVEN to moderate 180°C. Brush 2 shallow 20 cm round cake tins with oil or melted butter, line base and sides with baking paper.
1 Sift flour three times onto a sheet of greaseproof paper. Using electric beaters, beat eggs and sugar in a large mixing bowl for 6 minutes until thick, pale and increased in volume.
2 Using a metal spoon, fold in flour in two batches quickly and lightly until ingredients are just combined. Add the melted butter with the second batch, discarding any white sediment in the butter. Spread mixture evenly into prepared tins, bake for 20 minutes, until lightly golden and springy to touch. Leave cakes in tins for 2 minutes before turning out onto a wire rack to cool.
3 To make Filling: Combine cornflour with a little of the water in a small bowl to make a smooth paste. Place remaining water, juice, rind and sugar in a small pan; stir over medium heat without boiling until sugar has dissolved. Add cornflour mixture; stir constantly until mixture boils and

thickens. Cook, stirring, for another minute. Remove from heat, add egg yolks and butter, stir until well combined. Transfer to bowl, cover surface with plastic wrap; cool completely.

4 To make Topping: Place chocolate in a medium mixing bowl. Place cream in a small pan, bring to the boil. Pour hot cream over chocolate and stir until mixture is melted and smooth. Set aside to cool until just thick enough to whip. Using electric beaters, beat until soft peaks form.

5 To make Decoration: Peel wide strips of rind from lemon and, using a small sharp knife, remove all white pith. Cut star shapes from rind using a small cutter. Combine water and sugar in small pan. Stir constantly over medium heat until sugar is completely dissolved; add rind and bring to boil. Reduce heat to low and simmer, uncovered, 5 minutes. Remove rind with tongs and place on a wire rack to drain and cool. Spread melted chocolate about 1 cm thick onto a marble or laminex board; smooth surface. When just set, shave wide curls from chocolate using a sharp, flat-bladed knife or handyman's scraper.

6 To assemble Gateau: Using a serrated knife, cut cakes in half horizontally. Place one cake layer on serving plate. Spread the cake evenly with filling. Continue layering cake and filling, ending with a cake layer on top. Spread top and sides of cake with Topping, decorate with white chocolate curls and lemon rind stars.

COOK'S FILE

Storage time: Cake may be made up to a day in advance. Gateau may be assembled up to 8 hours in advance. Refrigerate during hot weather.

BANANA CARAMEL TART

Preparation time: 35 minutes +
  50 minutes refrigeration
Total cooking time: 40 minutes
Serves 8

1 1/4 cups plain flour
2 tablespoons icing sugar
3/4 cup ground walnuts
80 g butter, chopped
1/4 cup iced water

Filling
400 g condensed milk
30 g butter
1 tablespoon golden syrup
2 medium bananas, sliced
1 cup cream, whipped
1/2 cup pure thick cream
2 medium bananas, sliced, extra
50 g dark chocolate, melted

➤ SIFT FLOUR and icing sugar into a large mixing bowl.

1 Add walnuts and butter; rub butter into flour until fine and crumbly. Add almost all water, mix with flat-bladed knife to a firm dough; add more water if needed. Turn onto lightly floured surface, press together until smooth. Roll out and ease into 23 cm flan tin; trim edges. Cover with plastic wrap and refrigerate for 20 minutes.

2 Preheat oven to moderate 180°C. Cover pastry-lined tin with a sheet of greaseproof paper, spread dried beans or rice over paper. Bake 15 minutes, discard paper and beans. Return pastry to oven for 20 minutes, until lightly golden. Set aside to cool completely.

3 To make Filling: Place condensed milk, butter and syrup in a small, heavy-based pan. Stir constantly over medium heat 5 minutes, until it boils and thickens and turns a light caramel colour; cool slightly. Arrange sliced banana over pastry, pour caramel over; smooth with the back of a spoon. Refrigerate for 30 minutes.

4 Using a metal spoon, gently fold creams together. Drop dollops over caramel, arrange slices of banana on top. Drizzle with melted chocolate.

COOK'S FILE

Storage time: Tart may be refrigerated up to 1 hour before serving. Brush lemon juice on bananas.

1

2

3

4

RICOTTA CREPES WITH ORANGE SAUCE

Preparation time: 40 minutes
Total cooking time: 30 minutes
Serves 4

Crepes
2/3 cup plain flour
pinch salt
1 egg, lightly beaten
1 1/3 cups milk

Filling
1/4 cup sultanas
1 cup orange juice
200 g ricotta cheese
1 teaspoon finely grated
    orange rind
1/4 teaspoon vanilla essence

Orange Sauce
50 g butter
1/4 cup caster sugar
1 tablespoon Grand Marnier

➤ SIFT FLOUR and salt into a medium mixing bowl.

1 Make a well in the centre. Add combined egg and milk gradually. With wire whisk, beat until all liquid is incorporated and batter is free of lumps. Leave, covered with plastic wrap, for 30 minutes. Pour 2–3 tablespoons onto lightly greased crepe or non-stick frypan; swirl evenly over base to make a 16-cm round. Cook over medium heat 1–2 minutes or until underside is golden. Turn crepe, cook other side 30 seconds. Transfer to plate. Repeat with remaining batter, greasing pan lightly between crepes. Stack crepes with sheets of waxed paper between each. Preheat oven to moderately slow 160°C.

2 To make Filling: Place sultanas in bowl, cover with orange juice; soak for 15 minutes. Drain, reserving juice. Place ricotta, rind, essence and sultanas in a medium bowl and stir to combine. Place large tablespoonsful of mixture at edge of each crepe, fold in half and then half again. Place 2 filled crepes on each ovenproof serving plate, bake 10 minutes.

3 To make Orange Sauce: Melt butter and sugar in small pan over low heat. Add reserved juice and stir over medium heat without boiling until sugar dissolves. Bring to boil, simmer 10 minutes to reduce slightly. Stir in Grand Marnier. Cool 3–4 minutes, pour over warmed, filled crepes. Serve at once, with poached orange segments, if desired.

COOK'S FILE

Storage time: Crepes may be cooked up to 4 hours in advance, cover and refrigerate until required. Fill and heat close to serving time.

BANANA CHOC-CHIP PIZZA

Preparation time: 20 minutes + 1 hour
  standing
Total cooking time: 25 minutes
Serves 6–8

2 teaspoons dried yeast
2 teaspoons sugar
1/3 cup warm water
1 1/2 cups plain flour
25 g soft butter
1 egg, lightly beaten

Topping
30 g butter
2 tablespoons brown sugar

3 large bananas
2 tablespoons dark choc bits
2 tablespoons crushed
  macadamia nuts

➤ COMBINE YEAST, sugar and water in a small bowl. Stand, covered with plastic wrap, for 10 minutes, until mixture is foamy.

1 Sift flour into large bowl, make a well in centre. Add yeast mixture, butter and egg; mix with a knife to a soft dough. Turn onto lightly floured surface, knead 5 minutes, until smooth and elastic. Place in oiled bowl, cover with plastic wrap and leave in warm place 1 hour or until doubled in size.

2 Preheat oven to moderately hot 210°C. Brush a 30 cm pizza tray with melted butter. Knead dough again for 1 minute, roll out to a 26 cm round. Place onto prepared tray, tuck edges under to form a rim.

3 To make Topping: Combine butter and sugar in a small pan, stir until butter has melted and sugar has dissolved. Spread onto pizza base (mixture will separate a little). Cut bananas diagonally into 5 mm slices, arrange over base. Sprinkle choc bits and nuts over banana. Bake for 25 minutes, until pizza crust is golden brown. Serve warm. Decorate with strawberries, if desired.

COOK'S FILE

Storage time: Pizza is best made just before serving.

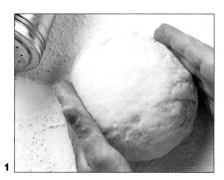

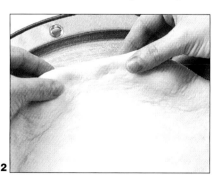

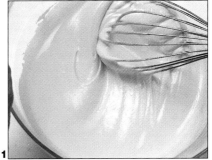

1

2

3

4

BLACK STICKY RICE WITH COCONUT ICE-CREAM

Preparation time: 45 minutes + 6 hours
 freezing
Total cooking time: 40 minutes
Serves 6

Coconut Ice-cream
1 cup cream
2 cups coconut cream
6 egg yolks
3/4 cup caster sugar

Black Sticky Rice
1 cup black rice, washed and
 soaked for 1 hour
2 cm piece fresh ginger, cut into
 2 slices
5 cups water
1/2 cup brown sugar
1/3 cup lime juice
2 teaspoons finely grated lime rind
3 mangoes

➤ COMBINE CREAM and coconut cream in a small pan.

1 Stir over medium heat until mixture just comes to boil; remove from heat. Place yolks and sugar in medium mixing bowl. With wire whisk, beat for 1 minute, until pale and thickened slightly. Pour warm cream mixture over yolks, whisking continuously.

2 Return mixture to pan. Stir over low heat 8 minutes or until mixture thickens slightly; do not boil. Pour into a shallow metal tray. Cover with plastic wrap, freeze about 4 hours, until just firm. Transfer to large mixing bowl, beat with electric beaters until smooth. Freeze for another 2 hours, until firm.

3 To make Rice: Drain rice, place in medium pan. Add ginger and water, bring to boil and simmer, uncovered, 30 minutes, until tender. Add more boiling water, if necessary, to keep rice covered. Drain.

4 Combine sugar and juice in clean pan. Stir over medium heat until sugar dissolves. Add rice and rind; cook, stirring, over low heat until the liquid evaporates and the mixture is thick and sticky. Transfer to a bowl and cool completely. Serve with Coconut Ice-cream and sliced fresh mango or other fruits, if desired.

COOK'S FILE

Storage time: Ice-cream can be made up to 2 days in advance; cover tightly in the freezer. The rice can be made up to 8 hours in advance.

Fast Fruit Finishes

BRIOCHE WITH WARM PEACHES

Cut 4 thick slices from day-old brioche and lightly toast one side. Brush untoasted side with melted butter, top with sliced peaches, dust thickly with icing sugar. Return to grill 3–4 minutes, until peaches are warmed through. Dust with more icing sugar, serve with vanilla ice-cream. Serves 4.

HOT ORANGE DATES

Slit the sides of 16 (about 300 g) fresh dates, remove stones. Heat 50 g butter in frypan, add dates and 1/4 cup orange juice. Cook over medium heat for 3 minutes, stirring and turning dates. Add 1/4 cup Grand Marnier, stir 2 minutes. Serve immediately with a dollop of fresh ricotta. Serves 4.

CARAMELISED APPLES

Peel, core and thickly slice 4 large cooking apples. Heat 50 g butter in frypan, stir in 1/4 cup brown sugar and 1 teaspoon ground ginger. Add apples and stir to coat with butter mixture. Cover and cook for 10 minutes over medium heat, stirring occasionally. Remove apples with a slotted spoon; keep warm. Add 1/2 cup cream to pan and stir to combine. Bring to the boil and cook for 2–3 minutes until volume has reduced slightly. Serve drizzled over apples. Serves 4.

CITRUS PASSIONFRUIT SYLLABUB

Whip 1 1/2 cups of cream lightly, then add 1/4 cup sifted icing sugar and beat until firm peaks form. Fold in 2/3 cup passionfruit pulp and 2 teaspoons finely grated orange or lemon rind; refrigerate until required. Spoon mixture into four dessert glasses and garnish with fine strips of rind. Serve with wafer biscuits. Serves 4.

SPONGE WITH BERRIES AND ICE-CREAM

Place 300 g fresh, or thawed frozen, berries in a small pan. Add 2–3 tablespoons caster sugar, stir gently over medium heat until sugar has dissolved and mixture has warmed through. Place a wedge of purchased sponge cake onto each serving plate, drizzle generously with berries and top with a scoop of good vanilla ice-cream. Serves 4.

QUICK ITALIAN TRIFLE

Cut 8 apricots in half, remove stones and slice the flesh. Roughly chop 12 amaretti biscuits. Fold together 1 cup mascarpone and 1 cup whipped cream. Layer apricot, biscuits and the cream mixture into 4 dessert glasses, sprinkling with a little Marsala between the layers. Refrigerate for 15–30 minutes to allow the biscuits to soften and the flavours to develop. Serves 4.

BAKED CHOCOLATE BANANAS

Slit 4 large bananas lengthways, leaving the skins on. Lay each on a piece of foil. Roughly chop 100 g Toblerone® and press some into centre of each banana. Close foil and cook on moderately hot barbecue 10–15 minutes. Open foil, fold down sides to form a 'bowl'; open skin slightly. Top with cream or ice-cream and eat straight from the skin. These can also be cooked in a moderate oven. Serves 4.

EASY NECTARINE BRULEE

Slice 8 nectarines thickly; divide between 4 serving bowls. Top with very cold, thick cream, spread slightly to cover fruit. Combine 1/2 cup sugar with 1/4 cup water in small pan. Stir over low heat without boiling until sugar has completely dissolved. Bring to boil, simmer until toffee turns golden brown—about 10 minutes. Remove from heat, wait until the bubbles have almost subsided then carefully drizzle hot toffee over cream. Cool for a minute before serving. Serves 4.

Clockwise from top left: Hot Orange Dates, Sponge with Berries and Ice-Cream, Baked Chocolate Bananas, Easy Nectarine Brulée, Quick Italian Trifle, Citrus Passionfruit Syllabub, Caramelised Apples and Brioche with Warm Peaches

HOT MOCHA SOUFFLE

Preparation time: 25 minutes
Total cooking time: 45 minutes
Serves 4–6

1 tablespoon caster sugar
40 g butter
2 tablespoons plain flour
3/4 cup milk
1 tablespoon instant espresso-
    style coffee powder
1 tablespoon hot water
2 tablespoons caster sugar,
    extra
100 g dark chocolate, melted
4 eggs, separated
icing sugar, for dusting

➤ PREHEAT OVEN to moderate 180°C.

1 Brush a 5-cup capacity soufflé dish with oil or melted butter. Sprinkle sugar in dish, turn dish to coat base and sides evenly; shake out excess. Wrap a double thickness of baking paper around dish to sit 3 cm above rim; tie securely with string.

2 Melt the butter in a medium pan, add flour. Stir over low heat for 2 minutes or until the mixture is lightly golden. Add milk gradually to pan, stirring between each addition until mixture is smooth.

3 Stir constantly over medium heat until the mixture boils and thickens. Boil for another minute, then remove from heat. Transfer to a large mixing bowl. Dissolve the coffee powder in hot water, add to the milk mixture with sugar, melted chocolate and egg yolks; beat until smooth.

4 Using electric beaters, beat the egg whites in a clean, dry mixing bowl until stiff peaks form. Using a metal spoon, fold one third of the egg whites into the chocolate mixture to soften it slightly. Gently fold in the remaining egg whites. Spoon the mixture into the prepared soufflé dish. Bake for 40 minutes, until soufflé is well risen and just firm to the touch. Remove from oven, remove collar from dish. Dust soufflé with icing sugar and serve immediately.

COOK'S FILE

Storage time: Soufflé is best made just before serving time.

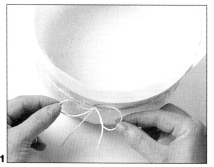

PEACH CHARLOTTES WITH MELBA SAUCE

Preparation time: 30 minutes
Total cooking time: 40 minutes
Serves 4

1 cup sugar
4 cups water
6 medium peaches, whole
1/3 cup peach liqueur
2 loaves brioche
100 g butter, melted
1/2 cup apricot jam, warmed
    and sieved

Melba Sauce
300 g fresh or thawed frozen
    raspberries
2 tablespoons icing sugar

➤ PREHEAT OVEN to moderate 180°C. Brush four 1-cup capacity ovenproof dishes with melted butter.
1 Combine sugar and water in large, heavy-based pan. Stir over medium heat until sugar completely dissolves. Bring to boil, reduce heat slightly, add peaches. Simmer, covered, 20 minutes. Drain and cool. Peel skins, slice flesh thickly. Place in a bowl, sprinkle with liqueur and set aside for 20 minutes.
2 Cut brioche into 1 cm-thick slices; remove crusts. With scone cutter, cut rounds to fit tops and bases of each dish. Cut remaining slices into 2 cm-wide fingers, trim to fit height of dish. Dip first round into melted butter and place in base of dish. Dip brioche fingers into melted butter, press around sides of dish, overlapping slightly. Line all the dishes in this manner.
3 Fill lined dishes evenly with peach slices, top with last round of brioche dipped in melted butter. Press to seal. Place dishes on baking tray, bake 20 minutes. Turn onto serving plates,

brush with jam and pour Sauce alongside. Serve with fresh berries, if desired.
4 To make Sauce: Process berries in food processor, add icing sugar to taste. Push through a fine sieve.

COOK'S FILE

Storage time: Peaches can be cooked, dishes lined with brioche and sauce made up to 6 hours ahead; refrigerate. Fill and bake charlottes close to serving time.

APPLE PIE

Preparation time: 30 minutes +
  20 minutes refrigeration
Total cooking time: 55 minutes
Serves 6

1¼ cups plain flour
¼ cup icing sugar
90 g butter
2 egg yolks, lightly beaten
1 tablespoon iced water

Filling
12 cooking apples
50 g butter
¼ cup brown sugar
1 teaspoon cinnamon
1 teaspoon mixed spice
1 egg white
1 teaspoon caster sugar

➤ PREHEAT OVEN to moderately hot 210°C. Brush rim of a 23 cm pie dish with melted butter.

1 Sift flour and sugar into large bowl; add butter. Rub butter into flour with fingertips until mixture is fine and crumbly. Add yolks, mix with knife to a firm dough, adding a little water if necessary. Turn onto a lightly floured surface, press together until smooth.

2 Roll pastry out on baking paper to a 25 cm round, cut 1 cm-wide strips from edge, cover rim of dish. Cover dish and remaining pastry with plastic wrap; refrigerate for 20 minutes.

3 Peel and core apples, cut into 8 slices each. Melt butter in large non-stick frying pan, add brown sugar and spices. Stir over medium heat until sugar dissolves; add apples, toss to coat with butter mixture. Cook, covered, 10 minutes, turning occasionally, until apples are soft but hold their shape. Remove lid, cook another 5 minutes, until liquid is reduced; cool.

4 Place cooled apple and any liquid into pie dish. Place pastry over fruit, pressing lightly onto rim. Trim edges, pinch together to seal. Decorate with trimmings. Brush with egg white and sprinkle with sugar. Bake 40 minutes, until golden. Serve warm with custard.

COOK'S FILE

Storage time: Prepare pie to end of step three 4 hours in advance. Assemble, bake close to serving time.

RICH CHOCOLATE SELF-SAUCING PUDDING

Preparation time: 20 minutes
Total cooking time: 45 minutes
Serves 6–8

1¹/2 cups self-raising
    flour
¹/4 cup cocoa powder
³/4 cup caster sugar
90 g butter, melted
³/4 cup milk
2 eggs, lightly beaten

Sauce
1¹/2 cups milk, extra
1 cup water
185 g dark chocolate, chopped

➤ PREHEAT OVEN to moderately hot 180°C. Brush a 9-cup capacity deep ovenproof dish with oil or melted butter.

1 Sift flour and cocoa into a large mixing bowl; add sugar, make a well in the centre.

2 Add butter and combined ³/4 cup milk and eggs. Using a wooden spoon, stir until all the ingredients are just combined and mixture is smooth; do not over-beat. Pour into prepared dish.

3 To make Sauce: Place extra milk, water and chocolate in a small pan and stir over low heat until chocolate has melted and mixture is smooth. Pour gently over pudding mixture. Bake for 45–50 minutes, until pudding is firm to the touch. Serve with cream or ice-cream and fresh fruit, if desired.

COOK'S FILE

Storage time: Pudding is best made just before serving.

CAPPUCCINO BROWNIES

Preparation time: 20 minutes
Total cooking time: 40 minutes
Serves 6

150 g butter
125 g dark chocolate
3 eggs
1¹/2 cups caster sugar
1 teaspoon vanilla essence
1 cup plain flour
¹/4 cup cocoa powder
2 tablespoons instant coffee
    powder
1 litre vanilla ice cream
1 teaspoon drinking chocolate

➤ PREHEAT OVEN to moderate 180°C. Brush a 28 x 18 cm shallow baking tin with oil or melted butter, line base with baking paper, extending over two sides.

1 Place butter and chocolate in small heatproof bowl. Stand bowl over a pan of simmering water and stir until melted and smooth. Remove from heat and cool slightly.

2 In a large bowl whisk eggs, sugar and essence together until well combined. Whisk in chocolate mixture, then stir in sifted flour, cocoa and coffee powder. Do not over-beat. Pour into prepared tin and bake for 40 minutes. Cool completely in tin, then refrigerate for 1 hour or until firm.

3 Lift the brownie from the tin using baking paper. Using an 8 cm round biscuit cutter, cut out 6 rounds while brownie is still warm. Place each round on a serving plate; top with 3 small scoops of ice-cream and dust lightly with drinking chocolate. Serve immediately. Garnish with fresh fruit, if desired.

COOK'S FILE

Storage time: Brownies may be made up to a day in advance. Assemble the dessert just before serving, adding the ice-cream scoops at the last minute.

Variation: Top with ice-cream of other flavours if you prefer.

TIRAMISU

Preparation time: 20 minutes
Total cooking time: Nil
Serves 6–8

3 cups strong black coffee,
    cooled
1/4 cup dark rum
2 eggs, separated
1/4 cup caster sugar
250 g mascarpone
1 cup cream, whipped
20 large savoyardi biscuits
2 teaspoons dark cocoa powder

➤ COMBINE COFFEE and rum in a deep glass or jug.

1 Using electric beaters, beat the egg yolks and sugar in a small bowl for 3 minutes until mixture is thick and pale. Add the mascarpone and beat until ingredients are just combined. Using a metal spoon, fold in the whipped cream.

2 Using electric beaters, beat egg whites until soft peaks form; fold quickly and lightly into cream mixture with a metal spoon.

3 Dip half the biscuits, one at a time, into the coffee mixture; drain off any excess and arrange in the base of a serving dish about 20 x 25 cm and 6 cm deep. Spread half the cream mixture over the biscuits.

4 Dip remaining biscuits and repeat layering with biscuits and cream mixture. Smooth surface and dust with cocoa powder. Refrigerate for 2 hours to allow the flavours to develop and until Tiramisu is firm. Serve with fresh fruit.

COOK'S FILE

Storage time: Tiramisu may be made up to 8 hours in advance. Refrigerate until required.

Variations: There are many adaptations of this classic Italian dish. Instead of rum, other alchohol-based flavourings, such as marsala or a favourite liqueur may be used. Decorate top with grated chocolate if you prefer.
Note: Tiramisu may be served before the two-hour refrigeration time is up but its flavour will improve considerably with standing, and it will be easier to serve.

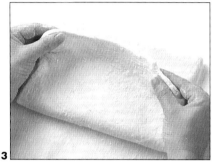

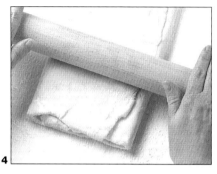

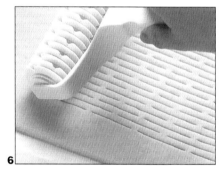

DATE STRUDEL

Preparation time: 40 minutes + 1 hour
  refrigeration
Total cooking time: 30 minutes
Serves 8

 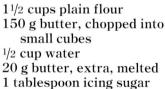

1¹/2 cups plain flour
150 g butter, chopped into
  small cubes
¹/2 cup water
20 g butter, extra, melted
1 tablespoon icing sugar

Filling
250 g fresh dates, pitted and
  roughly chopped
200 g ricotta
100 g cream cheese
2 tablespoons ground
  almonds
2 teaspoons finely grated
  orange rind

➤ SIFT FLOUR into a large bowl.
1 Stir in cold butter with a flat-bladed knife. Make a well in the centre of the flour, add almost all the water. Mix to a slightly sticky dough with a knife, adding more water if necessary. Gather dough into a ball.
2 Turn onto a floured surface and press together until almost smooth—do not overwork dough. Roll out on a sheet of lightly floured baking paper to a neat 20 cm x 40 cm rectangle, keeping the corners as square as possible. Fold the top third of the pastry down and fold the bottom third of the pastry up over it.
3 Make a quarter turn to the right so that the open edge of the fold is on the right. Re-roll pastry, dusting lightly with flour if sticky, to form a 20 cm x 40 cm rectangle, and repeat the folding step as above. Wrap the pastry in plastic wrap and refrigerate for 30 minutes.

4 Remove pastry from refrigerator and repeat previous step, giving a roll, fold, and turn twice more. Refrigerate another 30 minutes. (The folding and rolling give the pastry its flaky character.) Divide pastry in half and roll each half out on sheets of baking paper, making one sheet 15 cm x 30 cm and the other about 17 x 32 cm.

5 In a large mixing bowl, combine the dates, ricotta, cream cheese, almonds and orange rind. Spread filling in a flat mound on the smaller piece of pastry, leaving a 1-cm border around the edge.

6 Preheat oven to moderately hot 210°C. Using a pastry lattice cutter or small sharp knife, cut decorative slashes into the larger pastry sheet. Carefully lift onto filling; press edges to seal. Brush with melted butter and dust with half the icing sugar. Using baking paper, lift onto a flat oven tray and bake for 30 minutes, until crisp and golden. Remove from oven and dust with remaining icing sugar. Serve warm or at room temperature.

COOK'S FILE

Storage time: Strudel may be made up to 4 hours in advance.

Hint: Homemade flaky pastry is delicious and well worth the small effort it takes to make it properly. However, if time is short, frozen puff pastry may be used instead and will give a satisfactory result.

STRAWBERRY SWISS ROLL

Preparation time: 15 minutes +
  20 minutes standing
Total cooking time 10 minutes
Serves 6–8

3 eggs, separated
pinch salt
1/2 cup caster sugar
3/4 cup self-raising flour
2 tablespoons hot water
3/4 cup cream
1 tablespoon caster sugar
1/2 cup strawberry jam
250 g strawberries, quartered

whipped cream, strawberries,
  for decoration

➤ PREHEAT OVEN to moderately hot 200°C. Sprinkle 1 tablespoon sugar over a piece of baking paper 30 cm x 35 cm, resting on a clean tea towel. Brush a 26 cm x 30 cm Swiss roll tin with oil or melted butter; line tin with baking paper.

1 Beat egg whites and salt in a small bowl with electric mixer until soft peaks form; gradually add sugar and beat until dissolved. Add lightly beaten egg yolks, beat until thick. Transfer to a large bowl.

2 Fold in sifted flour and hot water. Spread mixture into prepared tin,

bake for 8–10 minutes or until firm and lightly browned. Turn onto sugared paper, peel paper from base. Using tea towel as a guide, roll up sponge loosely from narrow end. Set aside for 20 minutes or until roll has cooled; unroll. (This prevents sponge cracking when rolled with filling.)

3 Beat cream and sugar until soft peaks form. Spread roll with jam, top with cream and strawberries. Re-roll sponge, refrigerate until ready to serve. Decorate with cream and fresh, halved strawberries.

COOK'S FILE

Storage time: This dish may be made up to 4 hours before serving.

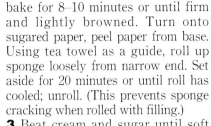

GOLDEN SYRUP DUMPLINGS

Preparation time: 20 minutes
Total cooking time: 10 minutes
Serves 6

1 1/2 cups self-raising flour
1/2 teaspoon baking powder
30 g butter, chopped
1 egg, lightly beaten
1/4 cup milk

Syrup
50 g butter

1/3 cup golden syrup
1 1/2 cups boiling water

➤ SIFT FLOUR and baking powder into medium mixing bowl; add butter.

1 Using fingertips, rub butter into flour until mixture is fine and crumbly. Add combined egg and milk, mix to a soft dough using a flat-bladed knife. Press together lightly into a ball. Divide into 12 equal portions and form into ball shapes.

2 Melt butter in a large pan, add golden syrup; stir over medium heat until butter melts and ingredients are combined. Pour in water, stir to combine.

3 Place dumplings gently into boiling syrup, cover and reduce heat to a simmer. Cook for 10 minutes, until a knife comes out clean when inserted into centre of one of the dumplings. Lift dumplings onto serving plates and drizzle with remaining syrup. Serve with cream or ice-cream and fresh raspberries, if desired.

COOK'S FILE

Storage time: Dumplings are best made just before serving.

Hint: A deep, heavy-based frypan with a lid is best for this recipe—an electric frypan is ideal.

Strawberry Swiss Roll (top) and Golden Syrup Dumplings

BELLINI SORBET

Preparation time: 20 minutes +
  freezing
Total cooking time: 2 minutes
Serves 6

2 cups caster sugar
4 cups water
5 large peaches
3/4 cup Champagne
2 egg whites

➤ COMBINE SUGAR and water in large pan.

1 Stir over medium heat without boiling until sugar has dissolved. Bring to the boil, add peaches and simmer for 20 minutes. Remove peaches from pan with a slotted spoon and cool completely. Remove 1 cup of the poaching liquid.

2 Peel skin from the peaches. Remove stones and cut flesh into chunks. Place in food processor and process until smooth. Add reserved liquid and Champagne and process briefly until combined.

3 Pour mixture into a shallow metal tray and freeze until just firm—about 6 hours. Transfer mixture to a large mixing bowl. Using electric beaters, beat until smooth.

4 Beat egg whites until soft peaks form. Using a metal spoon, gently fold beaten egg white into sorbet mixture. Return to metal tray and freeze until firm. Serve sorbet in scoops, with sliced fresh peaches and dessert wafers, if desired.

COOK'S FILE

Storage time: Sorbet may be made up to 2 days in advance; cover tightly.
Hint: To make sorbet in an ice-cream churn, pour mixture into machine after adding Champagne and churn until beginning to freeze. Add beaten egg white, continue churning until ready. It will be slow to freeze due to the amount of alcohol and sugar.
Note: Don't be tempted to use cheap Champagne or "sparkling wine" in this recipe—the difference will be noticeable. Use a wine of the same quality you would choose to drink.
Variation: Other soft stone fruits, such as nectarines or plums, can be used to make sorbet if you prefer.

ORANGE MACADAMIA TARTS

Preparation time: 40 minutes +
 15 minutes refrigeration
Total cooking time: 45 minutes
Serves 6

1¹/2 cups plain flour
100 g butter
3–4 tablespoons iced water

Filling
1¹/2 cups (200 g) macadamia
 nuts
¹/4 cup brown sugar
2 tablespoons light corn syrup
20 g butter, melted

1 egg, lightly beaten
2 teaspoons finely grated orange
 rind
pinch salt
icing sugar, for dusting

➤ PREHEAT OVEN to moderate 180°C.
1 Spread nuts in a single layer on a flat oven tray. Bake about 8 minutes, until lightly golden. Set aside to cool.
2 Place flour and butter in food processor. Using pulse action, process for 15 seconds or until fine and crumbly. Add almost all the water and process briefly until mixture comes together, adding more water if necessary. Turn onto lightly floured surface, press together until smooth. Divide dough into six equal portions.

Roll out, line six 8-cm fluted flan tins. Refrigerate 15 minutes. Cut sheets of greaseproof paper to fit pastry-lined tins, spread dried beans or rice evenly over paper. Place tins on an oven tray, bake 15 minutes. Remove from oven, discard paper and beans. Return to oven another 10 minutes until pastry is lightly golden. Cool completely.
3 Divide nuts equally between each pastry shell. With wire whisk, beat together sugar, syrup, butter, egg, rind and salt; pour over nuts. Bake for 20 minutes, until set and lightly browned. Dust with icing sugar.

COOK'S FILE

Storage time: Tarts may be made up to a day in advance.

Sweet Sauces and Custards

EASY FRUIT COULIS

Place 2 punnets of strawberries into food processor. Add about a tablespoon of icing sugar, according to taste, and process until liquid. Strain mixture through a sieve to remove seeds if desired. As a variation, blueberries, raspberries or the equivalent weight in soft fruits such as mangoes or kiwi fruit, can be used. Frozen berries are also suitable. Serve sauce over ice-cream, mousses, or with meringues and sliced fruit. Makes about 1 1/4 cups.

QUICK BUTTERSCOTCH SAUCE

Place 75 g butter, 1 cup brown sugar and 3/4 cup cream in a small pan. Stir over low heat until butter has melted and sugar has dissolved. Bring to the boil, reduce heat and simmer gently for 2 minutes. Makes about 1 1/2 cups.

HOT CHOCOLATE FUDGE SAUCE

In a small pan, combine 1 cup cream, 30 g butter, 1 tablespoon golden syrup and 200 g chopped dark chocolate. Stir over low heat until butter and chocolate have melted and the mixture is smooth. Serve sauce hot or at room temperature. Makes 2 cups.

JAM SAUCE

Combine 1 cup jam, 1 cup water and 1 teaspoon finely grated lemon rind in small pan. Use any jam you like. Stir over medium heat, reduce heat slightly and bring to boil, simmer 10 minutes. Add sugar to taste. Makes 2 cups.

SABAYON

Place 4 egg yolks, $1/4$ cup caster sugar and $1/2$ cup Marsala, sherry or sweet white wine in large bowl over a pan of barely simmering water. Beat with electric beaters 5 minutes until thick, light and foamy. Make close to serving time, as mixture will separate if left to stand. Makes $3^{1}/2$ cups.

CREME ANGLAIS

Whisk 3 egg yolks and 2 tablespoons sugar about 3 minutes until light and creamy. In small pan, heat $1^{1}/2$ cups milk until almost boiling, then pour onto egg mixture, stirring constantly. Return to pan, stir over low heat about 5 minutes, until thickened—do not boil or it will curdle. Stir in $1/2$ teaspoon vanilla essence. Makes about $1^{3}/4$ cups.

Clockwise from top left: Easy Fruit Coulis; Jam Sauce; Crème Anglais; Sabayon; Quick Butterscotch Sauce; Hot Chocolate Fudge Sauce

APPLE PEAR AND BLUEBERRY CRUMBLE

Preparation time: 15 minutes
Total cooking time: 30 minutes
Serves 6–8

3 apples, peeled
2 firm pears
1 tablespoon water
2 tablespoons sugar
250 g fresh blueberries

Crumble
90 g butter, melted
3/4 cup desiccated coconut
3/4 cup plain flour
1/2 cup soft brown sugar

➤ PREHEAT OVEN to moderate 180°C. Cut apples into 2 cm pieces. Slice unpeeled pears into thin slices, removing core.

1 Place apples and pears in a medium pan with the water, cover and simmer over low heat for 5 minutes. Stir in the sugar, cover and simmer for another 5–8 minutes or until the fruit is just tender. Remove from heat and stir in the blueberries.

2 Lightly grease a shallow baking dish with melted butter or oil. Spread the fruit mixture into the dish.

3 To make Crumble: Combine the butter, coconut, flour and sugar in a bowl. Stir until mixture is crumbly and butter is well distributed. Spread crumble mixture over the fruit mixture. Bake in preheated oven for 15–20 minutes or until top is golden and fruit is heated through. Serve with cream or ice-cream and sliced kiwifruit, if desired.

COOK'S FILE

Storage time: Apple, Pear and Blueberry Crumble is best made just before serving.
Variation: Other fruits can be used to make crumble if you prefer.

CHILLED LIME SOUFFLE

Preparation time: 35 minutes
Total cooking time: Nil
Serves 4

5 eggs, separated
1 cup caster sugar
2 teaspoons finely grated lime
   rind
3/4 cup strained lime juice
1 tablespoon gelatine
1/4 cup water
1 1/4 cups cream, lightly whipped
whipped cream, extra
shredded lime rind

➤ CUT FOUR strips of foil, fold each in half lengthways and wrap around four 1-cup capacity soufflé dishes, extending 4 cm above rim; secure with string. Brush inside top of foil with melted butter or oil.

1 Using electric beaters, beat egg yolks, sugar and lime rind in a small bowl for 3 minutes, until sugar has dissolved and the mixture is thick and pale.

2 Heat lime juice in a small pan then gradually add to yolk mixture while beating, until well mixed.

3 Combine gelatine with water in a small bowl to soften. Stand bowl in a larger heatproof bowl of hot water and stir until gelatine has dissolved. Add gradually to lime mixture, beating with beater speed on low, until combined. Transfer mixture to a large bowl, cover with plastic wrap and refrigerate for 15 minutes, until mixture is thickened but not set. Using a metal spoon, fold whipped cream into lime mixture until almost combined.

4 Using electric beaters, beat egg whites in a clean, dry mixing bowl until soft peaks form. Fold beaten egg white quickly and lightly into the lime

mixture until ingredients are just combined and there are no lumps of egg white remaining. Spoon the mixture gently into prepared soufflé dishes and chill until set. Remove the foil collar when ready to serve. Decorate with whipped cream and lime rind.

COOK'S FILE

Storage time: Chilled Lime Soufflé may be made up to 8 hours before being served.

PECAN PIE WITH BOURBON CREAM

Preparation time: 30 minutes +
 20 minutes refrigeration
Total cooking time: 1 hour 15 minutes
Serves 6

1¹/₂ cups plain flour
125 g butter, chopped
2–3 tablespoons iced water

Filling
2 cups pecans
3 eggs, lightly beaten
50 g butter, melted and cooled
²/₃ cup brown sugar
²/₃ cup light corn syrup
1 teaspoon vanilla essence
pinch salt

Bourbon Cream
1 cup cream

1 tablespoon icing sugar
2 teaspoons Bourbon

➤ PREHEAT OVEN to moderate 180°C.
1 Place flour and butter in food processor. Process using pulse action for 20 seconds or until mixture is fine and crumbly. Add almost all the water, process briefly until mixture comes together, adding more water if necessary. Turn onto lightly floured surface, press together until smooth.
2 Roll pastry out to a 35 cm round. Line a 23 cm flan tin with pastry, trim edges and refrigerate for 20 minutes. Pile pastry trimmings together, roll out on baking paper to a rectangle about 2 mm thick; refrigerate.
3 Cut a sheet of greaseproof paper large enough to cover pastry-lined tin. Spread a layer of dried beans or rice evenly over paper; bake for 15 minutes. Remove from oven, discard

paper and rice. Return to oven for another 15 minutes, or until lightly golden; cool completely.
4 To make Filling: Spread pecans over pastry base. In a large jug, whisk together eggs, butter, brown sugar, corn syrup, essence and salt until well combined; pour over nuts.

5 Using a fluted pastry wheel or small sharp knife, cut narrow strips from half the pastry. Cut out small stars with biscuit cutter from remaining pastry. Place decoratively over filling. Bake for 45 minutes, until firm. Cool completely and serve at room temperature with Bourbon Cream.

6 To make Bourbon Cream: Place the cream and icing sugar in a small bowl. Using electric beaters, whip until soft peaks form. Add the Bourbon and fold through with a metal spoon until it is just combined with the cream. Refrigerate until ready to use.

COOK'S FILE

Storage time: Pie may be made up to a day in advance and refrigerated until required.
Note: The pecan is native to North America and is much used in the cooking of the American South, as is Bourbon, the national drink.

45

CHOCOLATE TART WITH ESPRESSO CONES

Preparation time: 1 hour
Total cooking time: 5–10 minutes +
  refrigeration + freezing
Serves 8

Ice-cream Cones
1 litre good quality vanilla
  ice-cream, softened
1/4 cup instant coffee powder
1 tablespoon hot water

Tart Base
1 cup pecans
100 g dark chocolate biscuits
1 tablespoon cocoa powder
3 teaspoons brown sugar
1 tablespoon overproof rum
40 g dark chocolate, melted

Filling
200 g dark cooking chocolate
30 g butter
1/2 cup cream
3 egg yolks, lightly beaten
1 cup cream, whipped

➤ **To make Ice-cream Cones:**
Cover 8 large cream horn moulds with baking paper; secure with sticky tape. Transfer cones to inside of moulds. Stand, points down, in two mugs.
1 Using a metal spoon, fold combined coffee powder and water through ice-cream in a bowl; stir until smooth. Spoon into moulds, freeze overnight.
2 To make Tart Base: Grease a shallow, 23 cm round fluted flan tin. Process all ingredients in food processor, using pulse action, for 30 seconds or until even and crumbly. Press into base and sides of tin. Refrigerate overnight. Drizzle with melted chocolate.
3 To make Filling: Stir chocolate, butter and cream in heavy-based pan over low heat until melted and smooth; remove from heat, whisk in yolks. Transfer to bowl. Using a metal spoon, fold in whipped cream. Stir until smooth. Pour into tart base, refrigerate.
4 Place a wedge of Tart on each plate with an Ice-cream Cone, point up, alongside. Serve with thick cream.

COOK'S FILE

Storage time: This dish should be served immediately after assembling.

MANGO MILLE FEUILLE

Preparation time: 10 minutes
Total cooking time: 10 minutes
Serves 8

1 sheet ready rolled puff pastry
20 g butter, melted
2 teaspoons cinnamon sugar

Filling
125 g cream cheese
2 tablespoons caster sugar
1/2 cup sour cream
1 teaspoon vanilla essence
2 mangoes, peeled, sliced
icing sugar, for dusting

➤ PREHEAT OVEN to moderately hot 200°C. Line an oven tray with baking paper.
1 Cut pastry into eight 6 cm x 12 cm rectangles. Place pastry onto prepared oven trays. Brush with a little butter, sprinkle with cinnamon sugar. Bake in preheated oven for 8–10 minutes, or until puffed and golden; cool.

2 Using electric beaters, beat the cream cheese and sugar in a small bowl until smooth. Add sour cream and essence and beat until smooth and thick.
3 Cut each pastry in half horizontally. Spoon or pipe some cheese mixture onto each pastry base, top with mango slices, then pastry tops. Dust tops with sifted icing sugar.

COOK'S FILE

Storage time: Bake pastry a few hours ahead; fill just before serving.

PASHKA

Preparation time: 2 1/2 hours plus
  overnight refrigeration
Total cooking time: 15 minutes
Serves 8–10

1/2 cup (100 g) glacé pineapple
1/2 cup (100 g) glacé ginger
1/3 cup (60 g) mixed peel
1/4 cup (60 g) sultanas
2 tablespoons white or dark rum
100 g butter, softened
1/2 cup caster sugar
2 egg yolks
1/2 cup (60 g) slivered almonds,
  toasted
2 teaspoons finely grated lemon
  rind
2 teaspoons finely grated orange
  rind
2 tablespoons lemon juice
750 g fresh ricotta cheese,
  sieved
1/2 cup sour cream
whole blanched almonds and
  glacé apricots, for decoration

➤ CHOP PINEAPPLE and ginger.
1 In a medium bowl, combine pineapple and ginger with mixed peel, sultanas and rum. Soak 2 hours. Thoroughly wet a piece of muslin and wring out excess water. Use to line an 8-cup capacity pudding bowl.
2 Beat butter and sugar in medium bowl until light and creamy. Beat in egg yolks one at a time. Add almonds, rinds and lemon juice; mix well.

Transfer to large bowl. Fold in cheese, sour cream and fruit mixture.
3 Press mixture into prepared basin; fold edges of cloth over top. Cover top with plastic wrap, place a saucer on top and weigh down with a can placed on top of saucer. Place bowl on a plate and refrigerate overnight. Turn out of basin and peel away muslin. Place on serving plate with smaller end facing up. Decorate with almonds and glacé apricots. Serve small wedges to serve.

COOK'S FILE

Storage time: This will keep for up to 2 days in the refrigerator.
Hint: If muslin is unavailable, use a new 'Chux' type cloth.
Note: Pashka is a traditional Russian Easter dish.

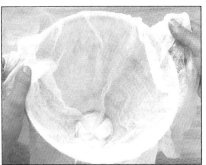

PLUM COBBLER

Preparation time: 15 minutes
Total cooking time: 45 minutes
Serves 6–8

750 g fresh blood plums
1 tablespoon water
1/4 cup caster sugar

Cobbler Topping
1 cup self-raising flour
1/2 cup plain flour
1/4 cup caster sugar
125 g butter, chopped
1 egg
1/2 cup milk
icing sugar, for dusting

➤ PREHEAT OVEN to moderate 180°C. Lightly grease an 8-cup capacity baking dish. Cut plums into quarters; remove seeds.
1 Place plums in medium pan, add water and sugar. Stir, uncovered, over low heat 5 minutes or until sugar dissolves and fruit softens slightly.

Spread plum mixture in prepared dish.
2 Sift flours into bowl; add sugar, stir. Rub in butter with fingertips until mixture is fine and crumbly. Combine egg and milk, whisk until smooth. Stir into flour mixture.
3 Place large spoonfuls of mixture on top of plums. Bake for 30–40 minutes or until golden and cooked through. Dust with icing sugar before serving.

COOK'S FILE

Storage time: Cook pudding just before serving.

Pashka (top) and Plum Cobbler

SPICED BAKED APPLES

Preparation time: 20 minutes
Total cooking time: 45 minutes
Serves 4

4 medium Granny Smith apples
1/4 cup raw sugar
1/4 cup (50 g) figs, chopped
1/4 cup (35 g) dried apricots,
   chopped

1/4 cup (30 g) slivered almonds
1 tablespoon apricot jam
1/4 teaspoon ground cardamom
1/4 teaspoon ground cinnamon
30 g butter

➤ PREHEAT OVEN to 180°C. Brush
a square, deep ovenproof dish with
melted butter.
1 Peel the apples and remove the
cores. Gently roll each apple in sugar.
In a medium bowl, combine figs,

apricots, almonds, jam and spices.
2 Fill each apple with the fruit mixture. Place apples in prepared dish.
Dot with pieces of butter.
3 Bake for 35–40 minutes or until
apples are tender. Serve warm with
cream or ice-cream.

COOK'S FILE

Storage time: Baked apples are best
prepared and baked just before
being served.

COCONUT CAKE WITH LEMON SYRUP

Preparation time: 10 minutes
Total cooking time: 1³/4 hours
Serves 8–10

250 g butter
1³/4 cups caster sugar
7 eggs, lightly beaten
1²/3 cups self-raising flour
4 cups desiccated coconut

Syrup
2 cups caster sugar
¹/2 cup lemon juice
¹/2 cup water
2 teaspoons finely grated
    lemon rind
1 small lemon, finely
    sliced
icing sugar, for
    dusting

➤ PREHEAT OVEN to moderate 160°C. Brush a 26 cm springform pan with melted butter or oil, line base with baking paper.
1 Place butter and sugar in a large bowl, beat on high speed until light and fluffy. Add eggs gradually, beating well after each addition.
2 Gently fold the sifted flour and coconut into the egg mixture. Pour into prepared pan. Bake for 1¹/2 hours, until just firm. (The cake may dip slightly in the centre.)
3 Combine sugar, lemon juice, water and lemon rind in a heavy-based pan. Cook over low heat, stirring constantly until sugar dissolves. Boil syrup without stirring for 12 minutes or until slightly thickened.
4 Remove cake from oven, pour hot syrup evenly over hot cake, reserving about ¹/2 cup of syrup. Leave in pan to cool completely. Add sliced lemon to remaining syrup and cook over low

heat for 5 minutes. Decorate cake with glazed lemon slices. Dust with icing sugar to serve.

COOK'S FILE

Storage time: Coconut Cake will keep for up to 2 days in an airtight container.
Variation: Orange juice and orange rind may be substituted for lemon juice and lemon rind, to make the syrup, if you prefer.

CHOCOLATE HAZELNUT TORTE

Preparation time: 1 hour + overnight refrigeration
Total cooking time: 1 hour
Serves 10–12

6 eggs
2 tablespoons Frangelico liqueur
500 g dark cooking chocolate, melted
1¹/₂ cups ground hazelnuts
1 cup cream, whipped

Topping
12 whole hazelnuts
200 g dark cooking chocolate
³/₄ cup cream
1 tablespoon Frangelico

➤ PREHEAT OVEN to slow 150°C. Brush a 20 cm round cake tin with melted butter or oil, line base and sides with baking paper.

1 Break eggs into a large heatproof bowl; add Frangelico. Stand over a pan of barely simmering water. Using electric beaters, beat on high speed for 7 minutes, until mixture is light and foamy. Remove from heat.

2 Using a metal spoon, quickly and lightly fold melted chocolate and nuts into egg mixture until just combined. Fold in whipped cream and pour into prepared tin. Place tin into a shallow baking dish. Pour in enough hot water to come halfway up the side of tin.

3 Bake for 1 hour, until just set; remove tin from baking dish. Cool to room temperature, cover with plastic wrap and place in refrigerator overnight.

4 Cut a 17 cm circle from a sheet of heavy cardboard. Invert chilled cake onto disc, so that the smooth base of cake becomes the top. Place on a wire rack over a flat baking tray, remove the paper and return cake to room temperature before decorating.

5 Place hazelnuts on a tray, bake in moderate 180°C oven for 8 minutes. Cool and rub off any loose skins. Combine chocolate, cream and

Frangelico in a small heatproof bowl. Heat gently over a pan of simmering water or in the microwave until melted and smooth. Transfer to a jug.

6 Using a little of the chocolate mixture, attach hazelnuts around edge of cake. Pour chocolate mixture over cake in centre, tilting slightly to cover the cake and nuts evenly. Use a flat-bladed knife to smooth over sides. Refrigerate until topping has set and cake is firm. Carefully transfer to serving plate with two long, flat-bladed knives. Cut into thin wedges to serve.

NUTMEG DATE CAKE

Preparation time: 25 minutes
Total cooking time: 55 minutes
Serves 8

2 cups brown sugar
2 cups plain flour
2 teaspoons baking powder
125 g cold butter, chopped
1 teaspoon bicarbonate soda
3/4 cup milk
2 eggs, beaten
1 1/2 teaspoons ground nutmeg
375 g packet dried dates,
    roughly chopped

2 tablespoons brown sugar
icing sugar, for dusting
thick pure cream

➤ PREHEAT OVEN to moderate 180°C. Brush a 22 cm springform pan with melted butter or oil; line base with baking paper.
1 Place the brown sugar, flour and baking powder in a food processor. Using pulse button, process for 10 seconds. Add butter and process for another 10 seconds until mixture resembles fine crumbs. Press half the mixture into the base of prepared tin.
2 Dissolve soda in milk; add eggs and nutmeg and whisk. Pour mixture into

remaining brown sugar and flour mixture and process for another 10 seconds. Pour into cake tin and scatter half the dates over the top. Bake for 55 minutes. Remove from oven, cool in tin 10 minutes before cooling completely on a wire rack.
3 Place remaining dates on top of cake, sprinkle with brown sugar and place under a very hot grill for about 1 minute, or until sugar begins to melt; cool. Dust with icing sugar and serve with thick pure cream.

COOK'S FILE

Storage time: Store for up to 2 days in an airtight container.

TROPICAL MERINGUE

Preparation time: 10 minutes
Total cooking time: 1 1/2 hours
Serves 6–8

4 egg whites
1/4 teaspoon cream of tartar
1 cup caster sugar

Filling
300 mls cream
1/2 cup desiccated coconut
450 g can unsweetened crushed
    pineapple, drained
100 g chopped walnuts, toasted

1 tablespoon rum
icing sugar for dusting

➤ PREHEAT OVEN to slow 150°C. Line two baking trays with baking paper; draw two 22 cm circles on greaseproof paper.
1 Beat egg whites and cream of tartar until soft peaks form. Add sugar 1 tablespoon at a time, beating constantly between each addition until mixture is thick and glossy.
2 Spread meringue evenly over the circles. Bake 1 hour; reduce temperature to 100°C, cook another 30 minutes. Remove from oven and cool completely. Carefully peel away paper.

3 To make Filling: Using electric beaters, beat cream until soft peaks form. Gently fold in coconut, pineapple, walnuts and rum. Spread filling over one meringue circle; top with the other circle. Refrigerate for 15 minutes to allow meringue to soften slightly. Dust the top with icing sugar before serving and decorate with tropical fruits, if desired.

COOK'S FILE

Storage time: Meringue may be made up to 4 hours in advance.
Note: It is important to allow meringue to soften slightly to make cutting easier.

NUT TORTE

Preparation time: 10 minutes
Total cooking time: 45 minutes
Serves 6–8

200 g walnuts
150 g hazelnuts
4 eggs, separated
1/3 cup caster sugar
1 teaspoon baking powder
2 1/2 cups cream
2 teaspoons vanilla essence
75 g each walnuts and
    hazelnuts, extra, toasted and
    chopped
1 tablespoon freshly ground
    coffee

➤ PREHEAT OVEN to moderate 160°C. Brush a 22 cm springform pan with oil or melted butter; line base with baking paper.

1 Place the nuts in a food processor and process using the pulse action until nuts are finely chopped. In a medium mixing bowl, beat egg yolks and sugar until thick, creamy and pale. In a separate bowl, beat the egg whites until soft peaks form. Fold the yolk mixture, nuts and baking powder gently into the egg whites, using a metal spoon.

2 Pour into prepared pan and bake for 35–40 minutes, or until cake springs back when tested with a fingertip. Turn cake onto a wire rack and allow to cool completely.

3 Beat the cream with the vanilla essence until thick. Using a sharp knife, cut cake in half horizontally. Place one cake layer on a plate and spread with cream; place the second layer on top and spread the remaining cream over the top and side. Decorate side of cake with chopped toasted nuts. Pipe extra whipped cream around top edge of torte, if desired. Dust cream with ground coffee and decorate the top as desired (eg with chocolate-coated nuts or coffee beans). Refrigerate torte for 30 minutes before cutting and serving.

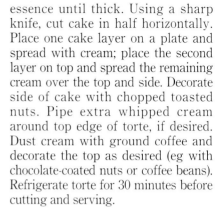
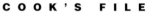

COOK'S FILE

Storage time: Nut Torte will keep in the refrigerator for up to a day.

BAKED PEARS IN SPICED CREAM

Preparation time: 20 minutes
Total cooking time: 1–1 1/2 hours
Serves 4

4 medium pears
2 1/2 cups cream
100 g chopped glacé ginger
2 tablespoons brown sugar
1 tablespoon finely grated
    orange rind
30 g butter, chopped

➤ PREHEAT OVEN to moderate 180°C. Brush a large ovenproof baking dish with oil or melted butter.

1 Peel the pears, cut them in half lengthways and remove the cores, leaving stem intact on one half of each pear. Place pears in prepared dish.

2 Place the cream in a small bowl and whisk with ginger, brown sugar and orange rind. Pour the cream evenly around the pears; dot the pears with butter.

3 Bake pears for 1 hour, or until they are tender when tested with the tip of a knife, and until the custard has thickened slightly. Serve immediately, with orange slices, if desired.

COOK'S FILE

Storage file: Baked Pears in Spiced Cream are best cooked and served immediately.

Variation: This dish is also delicious if made using sweet apples instead of pears.

Note: Do not leave pears exposed to the air after peeling or, like apples, they will turn brown. The pears should be ripe but firm, with no blemishes or bruising.

*Nut Torte (top) and
Baked Pears in Spiced Cream*

RUM BABA WITH FIGS

Preparation time: 40 minutes +
  2 hours standing
Total cooking time: 35 minutes
Makes 10
Serves 4–6

1$^1/_2$ cups plain flour
2 teaspoons dried yeast
$^1/_4$ teaspoon salt
2 teaspoons sugar
$^1/_3$ cup lukewarm milk
80 g butter
3 eggs, lightly beaten
2 cups water
1$^1/_2$ cups caster sugar
$^1/_3$ cup dark rum
$^3/_4$ cup apricot jam
2 tablespoons dark rum, extra
4–6 figs

➤ BRUSH 10 $^1/_2$-cup dariole moulds lightly with oil.

1 Place 1 tablespoon of the flour, and the yeast, salt, sugar and milk in a small bowl. Leave, covered with plastic wrap, in a warm place for about 10 minutes or until the mixture is foamy. Using your fingertips, rub butter into the remaining flour in a large mixing bowl, until the mixture is a fine crumbly texture.

2 Add the yeast mixture and the eggs to the flour mixture. Beat with a wooden spoon for 2 minutes, until smooth and glossy; scrape the mixture down the side of the bowl. Leave, covered with plastic wrap, in a warm place for 1$^1/_2$ hours, until well risen.

3 Preheat the oven to moderately hot 210°C. Using a wooden spoon, beat the mixture again for 2 minutes. Divide mixture evenly between prepared tins. Set aside, covered with plastic wrap, for another 30 minutes, until dough is well risen.

4 Bake for 20 minutes, until golden brown. Meanwhile, combine the water and sugar in a medium pan. Stir over medium heat without boiling until sugar has completely dissolved. Bring to the boil; reduce heat slightly and simmer, without stirring, for 15 minutes. Remove from heat, cool slightly and add rum.

5 Turn babas out onto a wire rack placed over a shallow oven tray. Brush warm babas liberally with warm rum syrup until they are well soaked; allow to drain. Strain excess syrup to remove any crumbs if necessary; reserve syrup.

6 Heat apricot jam in a small pan or in the microwave; strain through a fine sieve. Add extra rum, stir to combine and brush warm jam all over babas to glaze. To serve, place one or two babas on each plate, drizzle a pool of reserved syrup around them. Cut the figs in half and place on plate beside babas.

COOK'S FILE

Storage time: Rum Babas are best served on the day they are made.

Hint: If you do not have dariole or baba moulds, use empty baked bean tins. The 130 g size is best. Wash and dry the tins thoroughly and prepare as directed.

Note: It is important when working with a yeast dough such as the one used for babas that the temperature of the liquid used, as well as the surrounding temperature during rising, is neither too cold nor too hot. Measure ingredients accurately as they must be in the correct proportions. The yeast must not be stale. Oven temperature is also particularly important. If you have any reason to doubt the accuracy of your oven temperature readings, test with an oven thermometer so that you can make adjustments if needed.

4

5

6

ORANGE-CHOCOLATE CUPS

Preparation time: 25 minutes
Total cooking time: 8 minutes
Serves 6

125 g dark chocolate
1 1/2 cups milk
5 egg yolks
2 teaspoons finely grated orange
    rind
1/3 cup caster sugar
1/4 cup hot water
1 tablespoon gelatine
3/4 cup cream, softly
    whipped

whipped cream, extra, drinking
    chocolate, candied orange
    peel, for decoration

➤ CHOP CHOCOLATE finely.
1 Combine the milk and chocolate in a medium pan, warm over low heat until the chocolate melts. Using a wire whisk, beat the yolks with the rind and sugar until mixture is light and creamy. Pour the chocolate milk mixture into the egg mixture while stirring; return the mixture to the pan. Stir over low heat for about 5 minutes until the custard thickens slightly—do not allow to boil. Remove the custard from heat and stir it for 1 minute; transfer to a medium bowl.

2 Place water in a cup, sprinkle gelatine on top and mix well. Stand cup in a bowl of hot water and stir until gelatine has dissolved. Stir into the warm custard and mix well.
3 Allow mixture to cool and thicken slightly. Using a metal spoon, fold in whipped cream. Pour mixture into six individual dessert dishes. Refrigerate until firm. Decorate with whipped cream, chocolate and candied peel.

COOK'S FILE

Storage time: This dish may be made up to 6 hours ahead of time.
Hint: Whip the cream for this dish lightly—if too stiff it will not fold evenly through the mixture.

1

2

3

CRUNCHY MERINGUES WITH COFFEE CREAM

Preparation time: 30 minutes
Total cooking time: 2 hours
Serves 8

2 egg whites
¹/4 cup caster sugar
¹/4 cup demerara sugar

Coffee Cream
¹/2 cup strong black coffee
2 tablespoons caster sugar
2 teaspoons cornflour
1 tablespoon brandy
³/4 cup cream, lightly whipped

➤ LINE A flat baking tray with non-stick baking paper. Preheat oven to moderate 180°C.

1 Using electric beaters, beat egg whites in small, dry bowl until soft peaks form. Gradually add caster sugar, beating well after each addition until mixture is thick and glossy. Gradually beat in demerara sugar until it is evenly distributed throughout mixture (it will not dissolve).

2 Using a fluted nozzle, pipe 24 meringues onto prepared tray. Bake in preheated oven for 1 minute, then reduce oven temperature to slow 150°C and bake for another 1¹/2 hours or until meringues are crisp. Remove from oven, set aside for 1 minute, then

carefully lift meringues from paper and place on wire rack to cool.

3 To make Coffee Cream: Place coffee and sugar in small pan, bring to boil. In small bowl, combine cornflour and brandy to a smooth paste, add to pan, stirring until mixture thickens slightly; cool. Gradually fold in cream. To serve, arrange 3 meringues on each serving plate, with fresh fruit if desired. Dust meringues with icing sugar. Serve Coffee Cream separately.

COOK'S FILE

Storage time: Make meringues a day ahead, sauce close to serving time.
Variation: Serve meringues with fresh berries or a raspberry sauce.

1

3

HONEY CHOCOLATE MOUSSE

Preparation time: 20 minutes
Total cooking time: 10 minutes
Serves 6

225 g Toblerone®
¼ cup warm water
¾ cup cream
3 egg whites
1 punnet blueberries or raspberries

small block milk chocolate, at room temperature

➤ PLACE CHOCOLATE and warm water in a medium heatproof bowl over a pan of simmering water. Stir until melted. Remove from heat.

1 Using electric beaters, beat cream in medium bowl until soft peaks form. Beat egg whites in small bowl until stiff peaks form. Using a metal spoon, fold egg whites into cream.

2 Gently fold half the cream mixture into the chocolate mixture until both are combined, then fold in remaining cream mixture. Spoon into 6 individual dessert dishes or ramekins. Refrigerate for 6 hours.

3 Top the mousse with fresh berries. Make chocolate shavings by running a vegetable peeler firmly down the sides of a chocolate block. Sprinkle over the berries to decorate.

COOK'S FILE

Storage time: Mousse may be made up to 8 hours in advance. Refrigerate until required.

1

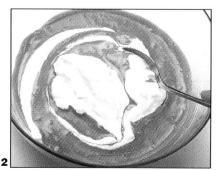

2

3

SPICY CHEESECAKE

Preparation time: 30 minutes
Total cooking time: 50 minutes
Serves 8–10

250 g butternut cookies
1 teaspoon mixed spice
100 g butter, melted

Filling
500 g cream cheese
2/3 cup caster sugar
1 teaspoon vanilla essence
1 tablespoon lemon juice
4 eggs, lightly beaten

Topping
1 cup sour cream
1/2 teaspoon vanilla essence
3 teaspoons lemon juice
1 tablespoon caster sugar
nutmeg for sprinkling

➤ LINE BASE of a 20 cm round springform cake tin with foil; brush with oil.

1 Place biscuits in food processor and process for 30 seconds or until finely crushed; transfer to a medium bowl. Add spice and butter and stir until all crumbs are moistened. Spoon into prepared tin and press firmly over base and sides. Refrigerate for 20 minutes or until firm.

2 To make Filling: Preheat oven to moderate 180°C. Using electric beaters, beat cream cheese until smooth. Add the sugar, essence and lemon juice and beat until smooth. Add the eggs gradually, beating well after each addition.

3 Pour the mixture into prepared tin and bake for 45 minutes or until cheesecake is just firm to touch. Remove from oven.

4 To make Topping: Combine sour cream, essence, juice and sugar in a

bowl. Spread over hot cheesecake. Sprinkle with nutmeg, return to oven for another 7 minutes. Cool, then refrigerate until firm. Decorate with whipped cream and grated orange rind, if desired.

COOK'S FILE

Storage time: May be refrigerated for up to 2 days.
Variation: Use gingernut bisuits to make base, if desired.

LEMON MERINGUE PIE

Preparation time: 30 minutes +
  30 minutes standing
Total cooking time: 10 minutes
Serves 8

1¼ cups plain flour
2–3 tablespoons icing sugar
125 g butter, chopped
3 tablespoons iced water

Filling
¼ cup cornflour
⅓ cup water
1 cup lemon juice
2 teaspoons finely grated lemon
  rind
¾ cup caster sugar
4 egg yolks
30 g butter, chopped

Topping
4 egg whites
¾ cup caster sugar

➤ PREHEAT OVEN to moderate 180°C.
1 Sift flour and icing sugar into large bowl; rub butter into flour with finger-tips for 2 minutes or until mixture is fine and crumbly. Add almost all water, mix to a firm dough, adding more liquid if necessary. Turn onto lightly floured surface, press together until smooth. Roll between 2 sheets of plastic wrap until large enough to cover base and side of 23 cm round pie dish. Line dish with pastry, trim and crimp edges; refrigerate 20 minutes. Place a sheet of greaseproof paper in pastry-lined dish, spread with dried beans or rice. Bake 10 minutes, remove from oven, discard paper and beans. Return to oven for another 10 minutes or until pastry is lightly golden. Leave to cool.

2 To make Filling: Combine cornflour with a little water to make a smooth paste. Combine remaining water, juice, rind and sugar in small pan, stir without boiling until sugar dissolves. Add cornflour mixture, stir until well combined. Stir over moderate heat until mixture boils and thickens. Simmer, stirring, 1 minute more. Remove from heat, whisk in egg yolks and butter. Transfer to bowl, cover surface with plastic wrap, cool.

3 To make Topping: Preheat oven to slow 150°C. Beat egg whites in small, dry mixing bowl with electric beaters until soft peaks form. Add sugar gradually, beating constantly until dissolved. Pour cold filling into cold pastry shell. Spread with meringue to cover, forming peaks. Bake for 20 minutes or until lightly browned.

COOK'S FILE

Storage time: Serve immediately.

PAVLOVA WITH FRESH FRUIT

Preparation time: 15 minutes
Total cooking time: 40 minutes
Serves 6–8

4 egg whites
1 cup caster sugar
3 teaspoons cornflour
1 teaspoon white vinegar
1 cup cream, whipped
2 kiwi fruit, sliced
250 g punnet strawberries, sliced
2 passionfruit

➤ PREHEAT OVEN to slow 150°C. Line an oven tray with baking paper. Mark a 20 cm circle on baking paper.
1 Place egg whites in large, dry mixing bowl. Using electric beaters, beat egg whites until soft peaks form. Gradually add the sugar, beating constantly after each addition. Beat for 5–10 minutes until sugar has dissolved. Fold in cornflour and vinegar.
2 Spread the meringue mixture on marked circle on prepared tray. Shape mixture evenly, running a flat-bladed knife around edge and over top of meringue. Run the knife up the edge of meringue mixture, all the way around, to make furrows. This will strengthen the pavlova as well as giving it a decorative finish.
3 Bake for 40 minutes or until meringue is pale and crisp. Turn off oven and cool pavlova in oven with the door ajar. Decorate with whipped cream and arrange kiwifruit and strawberries on top. Drizzle with passionfruit pulp and serve.

COOK'S FILE

Storage time: Meringue may be cooked up to 8 hours in advance. Serve within 1 hour of decorating.
Note: The meringue for pavlova is meant to be crisp outside and slightly soft inside.

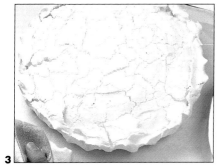

PARIS BREST

Preparation time: 40 minutes
Total cooking time: 1 hour 15 minutes
Serves 6–8

50 g butter
3/4 cup water
3/4 cup plain flour, sifted
3 eggs, lightly beaten

Filling
3 egg yolks
1/4 cup caster sugar
2 tablespoons plain flour
1 cup milk
1 teaspoon vanilla essence
1 punnet raspberries or
    strawberries
1 cup cream, whipped

Topping
125 g dark chocolate, chopped
30 g butter
1 tablespoon cream

➤ PREHEAT OVEN to moderately
hot 210°C. Brush a large pizza tray
with melted butter or oil. Line the tray
with baking paper and mark a 23 cm
circle on the paper.

1 Combine butter and water in medium pan. Stir over low heat until butter has melted and mixture boils.
Remove from heat, add flour all at
once and using a wooden spoon, beat
until smooth. Return to heat, beat
until mixture thickens and comes
away from sides of pan. Remove from
heat; cool slightly.

2 Transfer mixture to a large mixing
bowl. Using electric beaters, add the
eggs gradually, beating until mixture
is stiff and glossy. Place heaped tablespoons of mixture touching each other
using marked circle as a guide.
Sprinkle lightly with water. Bake for

20 minutes, reduce heat to moderate
180°C and bake for another
50 minutes. Turn off oven and leave
pastry ring to dry in oven.

3 To make Filling: Whisk yolks,
sugar and flour in a medium mixing
bowl until pale. Heat milk in pan until
almost boiling. Gradually add to egg
mixture, stirring constantly. Return
mixture to pan and stir constantly
over medium heat until mixture boils

and thickens. Cook for another 2 minutes, stirring constantly. Remove from heat, stir in essence, transfer to a bowl and cover surface with plastic wrap to prevent skin forming; leave to cool.

4 To make Icing: Combine chocolate, butter and .cream in a heatproof bowl. Stand bowl over a pan of simmering water and stir until chocolate has melted and mixture is smooth. Cool slightly.

5 To assemble, cut pastry ring in half horizontally using a serrated knife. Remove any excess dough that remains in the centre. Fold whipped cream through custard, spoon into base of pastry. Top with raspberries or halved strawberries. Replace remaining pastry half on top.

6 Using a flat-bladed knife, spread chocolate mixture over top of pastry. Leave to set.

COCONUT BAVAROIS

Preparation time: 20 minutes
Total cooking time: 10 minutes +
   2–3 hours refrigeration
Serves 6

1½ cups coconut milk
2 wide strips lemon rind, pith
    removed
4 egg yolks
½ cup caster sugar
1 tablespoon gelatine
¼ cup water
1 cup cream
1 pawpaw
4 ripe kiwifruit, pureed

➤ BRUSH SIX ¾-cup moulds lightly with oil.

1 Combine coconut milk and rind in medium pan. Bring to the boil, remove from heat and set aside for 30 minutes to allow the flavours to infuse.

2 Whisk egg yolks and sugar in a medium bowl until light and creamy. Reheat the coconut milk, then pour onto egg mixture, whisking continuously. Remove lemon rind and discard. Return mixture to pan, stir over very low heat for about 10 minutes, until mixture thickens slightly. Do not boil. Transfer to a bowl and cool until mixture is just warm.

3 Sprinkle gelatine over water in a small bowl, stand bowl in a larger heatproof bowl of hot water and stir with a fork until gelatine dissolves. Stir gelatine mixture into custard and set aside to cool to room temperature. Using electric beaters, beat cream until very soft peaks form. Using a metal spoon, fold cream into custard and stir gently until combined.

4 Pour mixture into prepared moulds, refrigerate 2–3 hours until set. To unmould, invert onto serving plates and place a well wrung-out wet warm cloth over each mould for a moment. Do not have the cloth too hot or the bavarois will melt. Lift away mould, arranged sliced pawpaw alongside and serve with pureed kiwi fruit. Garnish with kiwi fruit, if desired.

COOK'S FILE

Storage time: Store in refrigerator for up to 8 hours.

TRIFLE

Preparation time: 40 minutes +
  overnight refrigeration
Total cooking time: Nil
Serves 6

85 g packet port-wine jelly
1 sponge cake
1/3 cup cream sherry
2 tablespoons blackberry
  jam
425 g can pears, drained and
  chopped
425 g can peaches, drained and
  chopped

Custard
1/4 cup custard powder
1/4 cup caster sugar
2 cups milk
1 cup cream
1 teaspoon vanilla essence

Toffeed strawberries
1 cup sugar
1/4 cup water
1 x 250 g punnet strawberries
whipped cream, to serve

➤ MAKE JELLY as directed on the packet. Refrigerate until partly set.
1 Cut sponge into 1.5 cm cubes. Combine sherry and jam in small pan. Stir over low heat until jam melts. Remove from heat. Place half sponge cubes in a deep 12-cup capacity glass bowl. Brush with half sherry mixture. Top with remaining sponge, repeat with sherry mixture. Cover with plastic wrap, refrigerate.
2 To make Custard: Blend custard powder and sugar with a little milk in small bowl. Place remaining milk and cream in medium heavy-based pan. Add custard mixture. Stir over medium heat until the custard boils and thickens. Remove from heat and stir

in essence. Cover with plastic wrap to prevent a skin forming; cool.
3 Spoon partly set jelly on top of sponge. Top with fruit and custard. Decorate with whipped cream and toffeed strawberries.
4 To make Toffeed Strawberries: Line oven tray with foil. Stir sugar and water in medium heavy-based pan over medium heat without boiling until sugar completely dissolves. Brush crystals from side of pan with a wet brush. Bring to boil, reduce heat slightly; boil without stirring 15 minutes or until golden. Remove from heat. Dip strawberries in syrup, drain and place on tray.

COOK'S FILE

Storage time: Trifle may be stored for up to 8 hours in the refrigerator. Prepare the toffeed strawberries just before trifle is to be decorated but allow enough time for them to set.

CASSATA

Preparation time: 50 minutes +
  overnight freezing
Total cooking time: Nil
Serves 20

First layer
2 eggs, separated
1/3 cup icing sugar
3/4 cup cream
50 g flaked almonds, toasted
almond essence

Second layer
130 g dark chocolate, chopped
1 tablespoon dark cocoa
2 eggs, separated
1/3 cup icing sugar
3/4 cup thickened or pouring cream

Third layer
2 eggs, separated
1/4 cup icing sugar
1 cup thickened or pouring cream
60 g glacé cherries, halved
2 tablespoons chopped
  preserved ginger
220 g glacé fruit (pineapple,
  apricot, fig and peach), finely
  chopped
1 teaspoon vanilla essence

➤ LINE BASE and sides of a deep
20 cm square tin with foil.

1 To make first layer: Beat egg
whites with electric beaters until soft
peaks form. Add the icing sugar gradually, beating well after each addition.
In a separate bowl, beat cream until
firm peaks form. Using a metal spoon,
fold yolks and beaten egg whites into
cream. Add almonds and a few drops
of essence. Stir until combined. Spoon
into tin; smooth surface. Tap tin gently
on bench to level surface of mixture.
Freeze 30–60 minutes, or until firm.

2 To make second layer: Place
chocolate in heatproof bowl over pan
of simmering water; stir until melted.
Add cocoa, stir until smooth. Remove
from heat, cool slightly. Proceed as for
step 1, beating egg whites, icing sugar
and then cream. Using a metal spoon,
fold chocolate into cream. Fold in
yolks and beaten egg whites, stir until
smooth. Spoon over frozen first layer.
Tap tin on bench to level surface.
Freeze 30–60 minutes, until firm.

3 To make third layer: Proceed as
for step 1, beating egg whites, icing
sugar and then cream. With metal
spoon, fold yolks and egg white into
cream; stir in fruit and essence. Spoon
over chocolate layer in tin. Freeze
overnight. Slice and serve. Wrap
remainder in foil and return to freezer.

COOK'S FILE

Storage time: Store for up to 1 week,
tightly wrapped, in freezer.

DATE AND MASCARPONE TART

Preparation time: 50 minutes +
standing time
Total cooking time: 40–45 minutes
Serves 6–8

Pastry
1/2 cup rice flour
1/2 cup plain flour
2 tablespoons icing sugar
1/4 cup desiccated coconut
100 g marzipan, chopped
100 g chilled butter, chopped

Filling
8 (200 g) fresh dates, stones
removed

2 eggs
2 teaspoons custard powder
125 g mascarpone
2 tablespoons caster sugar
1/3 cup cream
2 tablespoons flaked almonds

➤ PREHEAT OVEN to moderate 180°C. Grease a shallow, 10 x 35 cm fluted loose-bottomed flan tin.
1 Process flours, icing sugar, coconut and marzipan in a food processor for 10 seconds or until combined. Add butter, process 10–20 seconds, or until mixture just comes together when squeezed. (Do not over-process.) Turn onto lightly floured surface, knead gently for 20 seconds. Cover and refrigerate for 15 minutes.
2 To make Filling: Cut dates into

quarters lengthways. Roll pastry, between two sheets of baking paper, large enough to line prepared tin. Ease pastry into tin; trim edge. Refrigerate 5–10 minutes. Cover pastry-lined tin with a sheet of baking paper, spread with dried beans or rice. Place tin on oven tray, bake 10 minutes. Remove from oven, discard paper and beans. Return to oven, bake another 5 minutes or until just golden; cool.
3 Arrange dates over pastry. Whisk together eggs, custard powder, mascarpone, sugar and cream until smooth. Pour over dates, sprinkle with almonds. Bake 25–30 minutes or until golden and just set; cool. Serve warm.

C O O K ' S   F I L E

Storage time: Serve immediately.

LEMON & LIME CAKE

Preparation time: 25 minutes
Total cooking time: 55 minutes
Serves 8–10

6 eggs, separated
1¹/₄ cups caster sugar
2 tablespoons finely grated lime
   rind
2 tablespoons finely grated
   lemon rind
¹/₄ cup lemon juice
¹/₄ cup lime juice
1 cup potato flour
1¹/₄ cups thickened cream,
   whipped
1 lemon
2 limes
¹/₄ cup caster sugar, extra

➤ PREHEAT OVEN to moderate
180°C. Brush a 23 cm springform pan
with melted butter or oil. Dust base
and sides with a little caster sugar,
then with potato flour.

1 Place egg yolks and sugar in a large
bowl. Using electric beaters, beat for
3 minutes until mixture is thick and
creamy. Add lime rind and lemon
rind, and lemon and lime juice. Beat
mixture briefly until ingredients are
just combined.

2 Add sifted potato flour. With clean
beaters, beat the egg whites in a small
bowl until soft peaks form; fold into
yolk mixture using a metal spoon.

3 Pour the mixture into prepared tin
and bake for 55–60 minutes until
golden and firm to the touch. Leave
cake in the tin for 5 minutes before
turning out onto a wire rack to cool
completely.

4 Using a serrated knife, cut cake in
half horizontally. Spread the bottom
layer with whipped cream; replace top
layer. Cut very thin slices of lemon
and lime, pat away excess moisture
with paper towel and coat the slices in
caster sugar. Arrange lemon and lime
slices on top of cake and serve.

COOK'S FILE

Storage time: Cake is best eaten on
the day it is made.
Note: Potato flour is a very dense,
starchy flour more often used as a
thickening agent than for baking. It
makes this delicious cake quite moist.

APPLE AND PECAN TART

Preparation time: 25 minutes
Total cooking time: 35 minutes
Serves 8

1/2 cup pecans
50 g butter
1/4 cup caster sugar
1 teaspoon finely grated lemon
    rind
1 egg, lightly beaten
2 tablespoons plain flour
3 green apples
10 sheets filo pastry
40 g butter, melted
icing sugar, to dust

➤ PREHEAT OVEN to moderate 180°C. Brush a 35 x 11 cm oblong flat tin with melted butter or oil.

1 Spread the pecans in a single layer on an oven tray and bake them for 5 minutes, until the nuts are lightly toasted. Remove tray from the oven, cool the nuts and chop them finely.

2 Place the butter, sugar, lemon rind and egg in a medium bowl. Using electric beaters, beat together until mixture is creamy. Stir in the flour and nuts.

3 Peel, core and thinly slice apples. Layer 10 sheets of the filo pastry in the prepared tin, brushing each sheet with melted butter before laying the next sheet on top. Spread the nut mixture evenly over the pastry base and lay the apple slices on top.

4 Fold the overhanging pastry over the filling and brush with butter. Trim one side of the pastry lengthsways and use it to crumple over the top of the tart. Bake for 45 minutes, until the tart is brown and crisp. Before serving, dust with icing sugar. Serve slices hot or cold with cream or ice-cream, if desired.

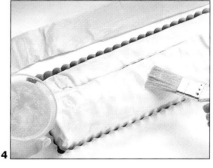

COOK'S FILE

Storage time: Apple Pecan Tart is best eaten on the day it is made.

Variation: Thinly sliced pears may be used instead of apples to make this tart. Green apples such as Granny Smith will give it a sharper flavour, but other apple varieties can be used if you prefer. Walnuts may replace the pecans. Toasting the nuts will improve their flavour and make them a little more crunchy.

DARK GINGER CAKE

Preparation time: 15 minutes
Total cooking time: 40 minutes
Serves 8

125 g butter
3/4 cup brown sugar
1/3 cup black treacle
1 1/2 cups plain flour
1 teaspoon cornflour
3 teaspoons ground ginger
1 teaspoon bicarbonate of soda
1 egg, lightly beaten
2/3 cup warm milk

➤ PREHEAT OVEN to moderately slow 160°C. Brush a 20 x 30 cm shallow tin with melted butter or oil, line base and sides with baking paper.
1 Place butter, sugar and treacle in a medium pan and stir over low heat until butter has melted, sugar has dissolved and mixture is smooth. Remove from heat and cool slightly.
2 Sift flours, ginger and soda into a large mixing bowl and make a well in the centre; add butter mixture, egg and milk. Stir with a wooden spoon until all ingredients are combined; do not over-beat.
3 Pour mixture into prepared tin and

bake for 40 minutes or until a skewer comes out clean when inserted into the centre of cake. Leave cake in tin for 5 minutes before cutting into squares or triangles. Serve warm with custard or thick cream, and fresh fruit, if desired. The top of the cake may be dusted with extra ground ginger, sifted icing sugar or a mixture of the two, if desired.

COOK'S FILE

Storage time: Cake may be cooled completely on a wire rack, and stored in an airtight container for up to 4 days.

1

2

3

NASHI CHEESECAKE SLICE

Preparation time: 25 minutes
Total cooking time: 50 minutes
Serves 8

250 g amaretti biscuits
80 g butter, melted

Filling
2 Nashi pears, peeled, cored and
   sliced
2 teaspoons lemon juice
250 g cream cheese
1/2 cup caster sugar
2 eggs, lightly beaten
1 tablespoon custard powder
1 teaspoon vanilla essence

➤ PREHEAT OVEN to moderate 180°C. Brush a shallow 20 cm square cake tin with oil or melted butter; line the base and sides with baking paper.

1 Place biscuits in food processor and process briefly to make fine crumbs. Add butter and process again until combined. Press firmly into base of prepared tin; refrigerate until firm.

2 Place pears in a single layer on a flat oven tray and brush with lemon juice. Bake for 10 minutes, until slightly softened. Cool and arrange over base.

3 Using electric beaters, beat the cream cheese and sugar in a small bowl until light and creamy. Add the eggs gradually, beating thoroughly after each addition. Add the custard powder and essence and beat until combined.

4 Pour cream cheese mixture over pears. Bake for 40 minutes, until set. Cut cheesecake into 8 slices and serve warm with cream or ice-cream. Garnish with kiwi fruit and shredded orange rind, if desired.

COOK'S FILE

Storage time: Nashi Cheesecake Slice is best eaten on the day it is made.

Note: The Nashi is a member of the pear family but looks more like an apple. It has a delicate flavour and a crisp rather than mushy texture.

Variation: Other varieties of pear may be used in this recipe, or try thinly sliced apples, if Nashi pears are not available.

MACERATED FRUITS WITH MASCARPONE

Preparation time: 20 minutes
Total cooking time: 10 minutes
Serves 4–6

2 oranges
1 cup raspberries
1 cup blueberries
2 tablespoons caster
    sugar
1/3 cup water
2 tablespoons sugar

➤ PLACE EACH orange on a board and cut a 2 cm-wide slice from each end—cut down to where pulp starts.

1 Remove rind in wide strips, including all pith and white membrane. Using a small, sharp knife, cut pith from rind and discard; cut the rind into thin strips.

2 Separate orange segments by carefully cutting between membrane and flesh. Combine orange segments and berries in a medium bowl, sprinkle with caster sugar and toss lightly. Cover and refrigerate.

3 Combine water and sugar in a small pan and stir over low heat without boiling until the sugar has dissolved. Bring to the boil, reduce heat and add the orange rind. Simmer for 2 minutes until rind is tender; cool. Reserve 1 tablespoon of rind, combine syrup and remaining rind with berry mixture. Spoon into goblets and garnish with reserved rind; serve with large dollops of mascarpone.

COOK'S FILE

Storage time: Fruit may be combined with syrup and refrigerated for up to 4 hours.

MINI TOFFEE PUFFS WITH LIQUEUR CREAM

Preparation time: 30 minutes
Total cooking time: 25 minutes
Serves 4–6

35 g butter
1/4 cup water
1/4 cup plain flour
1 egg, lightly beaten

Liqueur Cream
1/2 cup cream
1 tablespoon Grand Marnier

Toffee
1 cup caster sugar
1/3 cup water

▶ PREHEAT OVEN to hot 220°C. Line an oven tray with baking paper.
1 Combine the butter and water in a small pan. Stir over low heat until the butter is melted and the mixture just boils. Remove from heat and add the flour all at once. Using a wooden spoon, beat mixture until smooth. Return to heat then beat until mixture thickens and comes away from side of pan. Remove from heat, cool slightly. Transfer to small bowl. Using electric beaters, add egg gradually, beating until mixture is thick and glossy.
2 Drop teaspoonfuls of mixture about 4 cm apart on prepared tray. Bake for 10 minutes, reduce heat to 180°C and bake another 5–10 minutes, or until golden and well puffed. Pierce side of each puff to release steam. Turn off oven, return puffs to oven to dry; cool.
3 To make Liqueur Cream: Using electric beaters, beat cream until soft peaks form. Add Grand Marnier, beat until just combined. Place cream in piping bag fitted with a small plain nozzle. Pipe into puffs.

4 To make Toffee: Combine sugar and water in small pan. Stir over low heat until sugar dissolves, brushing down sides of pan occasionally. Bring to boil, simmer until golden. Quickly spoon over puffs and allow to set.

COOK'S FILE

Storage time: Make Toffee Puffs up to 6 hours in advance; store in airtight container. Fill and coat with toffee within 1 hour of serving.

AFTER-DINNER TREATS

At the end of a sumptuous meal, or at any time, offering small, sweet treats with coffee adds a touch of class—and how much more impressive (and satisfying) it is to make your own. After-dinner treats need not be elaborate: most are simple and fun to make. Some feature chocolate, the traditional partner for coffee, but in this chapter you will also find ideas for light, crisp delights like brandy snaps, amaretti, shortbread and even fortune cookies. Choose whichever sweet morsels will complement your menu or occasion and end on the perfect note.

FLORENTINES

Preparation time: 25 minutes
Total cooking time: 7 minutes each
Makes 24

1/4 cup plain flour
2 tablespoons chopped
    walnuts
2 tablespoons chopped flaked
    almonds
2 tablespoons finely chopped
    glacé cherries
2 tablespoons finely chopped
    mixed peel
75 g unsalted butter
1/4 cup soft brown sugar
180 g white chocolate melts

➤ PREHEAT OVEN to moderate 180°C. Line a 32 x 28 cm biscuit tray with baking paper.
1 Sift the flour into a medium bowl.

Add the walnuts, almonds, cherries and the mixed peel. Stir to combine these ingredients, then make a well in the centre. Combine the butter and sugar in a small pan. Stir over low heat until the butter has melted and the sugar has dissolved, then remove the pan from the heat. Add the butter mixture to the dry ingredients. Using a wooden spoon, stir until the two mixtures are just combined, being careful not to over-beat.
2 Drop heaped teaspoonsful of the mixture onto the prepared trays, leaving about 7 cm between each spoonful to allow for spreading. Press the mounds of mixture out to form neat 5 cm rounds. Bake the biscuits for 7 minutes. Remove the tray from the oven. While the biscuits are still soft, use a flat-bladed knife to push them into rounds, neatening the edges. Cool on the tray for 5 minutes before transferring to a wire rack and

allowing them to cool completely.
3 Place the chocolate melts in a heatproof bowl. Place the bowl over a pan of simmering (not boiling) water and stir gently until the chocolate has melted and is smooth. Using a flat-bladed knife, carefully spread the chocolate on the underside of the Florentines. Using a fork, mark decorative wavy lines in the chocolate while it is still soft. Place the biscuits chocolate-side up on a wire rack and leave them to set before serving.

COOK'S FILE

Storage time: Florentines are best made on the day of serving.
Variation: Use dark chocolate melts instead of white chocolate if you prefer, or decorate half the biscuits with dark chocolate and the other half with white. You could also drizzle the top with decorative lines of chocolate if you wish.

MIXED FRUIT AND NUT BALLS

Preparation time: 30 minutes +
 1 hour soaking
Total cooking time: 7 minutes
Makes 35

¹/4 cup sultanas
¹/4 cup finely chopped pecan nuts
1 tablespoon mixed peel
2 tablespoons chopped glacé
 ginger

1 tablespoon brandy
1 tablespoon light olive oil
375 g dark chocolate, chopped
125 g finely chopped toasted
 pecans

1 PLACE SULTANAS, pecans, peel and ginger in medium bowl. Add brandy and oil, stir well and leave to soak for 1 hour.
2 Place the chocolate in a small heatproof bowl. Place bowl over a pan of simmering water and stir until chocolate has melted.

3 Add fruit and nut mixture to melted chocolate. Refrigerate until firm enough to handle.
4 Roll teaspoonfuls of mixture into small balls. Roll each ball lightly in chopped nuts to coat. Place balls in refrigerator until firm. Serve in small paper confectionery cases.

COOK'S FILE

Storage time: Mixed Fruit and Nut Balls may be stored for up to 2 days in an airtight container in a cool, dark place.

TINY TUILES

Preparation time: 8 minutes +
  2 hours standing
Total cooking time: 5 minutes
  each tray
Makes about 40

1/3 cup plain flour
1/4 cup caster sugar
30 g unsalted butter, melted
1 egg white, lightly beaten
few drops almond essence

➤ BRUSH TWO 32 cm x 28 cm biscuit trays with melted butter or oil. Mark four 5-cm circles on baking paper, place pencil-side down on tray. Preheat oven to moderate 180°C.
1 Sift flour into medium mixing bowl; add sugar. Make a well in centre. Add butter, egg white and essence. Combine well using a wooden spoon.
2 Working on one tray at a time, spread 1/2 teaspoon of mixture into each marked circle. Bake 5 minutes or until lightly golden. Meanwhile, spread mixture onto other tray.

3 Remove from oven and leave on tray for 30 seconds. Carefully loosen and lift biscuits from tray and shape over a bottle or rolling pin while still soft. Work quite quickly as biscuits will become crisp as they cool.

COOK'S FILE

Storage time: Store biscuits in an airtight container for up to 2 days.
Hint: Cook only 3–4 biscuits at a time to allow enough time to mould them to shape before they cool—biscuits will become crisp on standing.

1

2

3

AMARETTI

Preparation time: 25 minutes +
  1 hour standing
Total cooking time: 15 minutes
Makes 40

1 tablespoon plain flour
1 tablespoon cornflour
1 teaspoon ground cinnamon
$3/4$ cup caster sugar
1 teaspoon grated lemon rind
1 cup (120 g) ground almonds
2 egg whites
$1/4$ cup icing sugar

➤ LINE TWO 32 x 28 cm biscuit tray with baking paper. Preheat oven to moderate 180°C.

1 Sift plain flour, cornflour, cinnamon and half the sugar into a large bowl; add lemon rind and ground almonds; stir to combine.

2 Place egg whites in small, dry mixing bowl. Using electric beaters, beat until firm peaks form. Add remaining sugar gradually, beating constantly until mixture is thick and glossy and all sugar has dissolved. Using a metal spoon, fold egg white mixture into dry ingredients. Stir until ingredients are just combined and mixture forms a soft dough.

3 Roll 2 level teaspoons of mixture at a time with oiled or wetted hands into a ball. Arrange on prepared tray, allowing room for spreading.

4 Sift icing sugar liberally over biscuits. Bake for 15 minutes or until biscuits are lightly browned. Transfer to wire rack to cool.

COOK'S FILE

Storage time: Store in an airtight container for up to 2 days.
Variation: Use orange rind instead of lemon rind, if desired.

DIAMOND CRISPS

Preparation time: 25 minutes
Total cooking time: 15 minutes
Makes approximately 30

125 g butter
1/2 cup caster sugar
1/2 teaspoon vanilla essence
2 tablespoons oatmeal
1 cup plain flour
1 tablespoon cocoa powder
100 g dark choc melts, melted

➤ PREHEAT OVEN to moderate 180°C. Brush an oven tray with melted butter or oil; line with baking paper.

1 Using electric beaters, beat butter and sugar in a small bowl until light and creamy. Add essence and beat until combined.

2 Transfer mixture to a medium mixing bowl. Add the oatmeal, and the sifted flour and cocoa powder; using a flat-bladed knife, mix to a soft dough. Turn dough onto a lightly floured surface and press together until smooth.

3 Roll out the dough to a thickness of 1 cm. Cut into 4 cm diamond shapes. Place shapes on prepared tray and bake for 10 minutes, or until crisps are golden brown. Cool completely on a wire rack. Pipe or drizzle chocolate over crisps.

COOK'S FILE

Storage time: Store Diamond Crisps for up to 3 days in an airtight container.

Variation: Use white choc melts instead of dark, if desired.

1

2

3

BRANDY SNAPS

Preparation time: 12 minutes
Total cooking time: 6 minutes
Makes 25

60 g unsalted butter
2 tablespoons golden syrup
1/3 cup soft brown sugar, lightly
   packed
1/4 cup plain flour
1 1/2 teaspoons ground ginger
100 g dark chocolate, melted

➤ PREHEAT THE OVEN to moderate 180°C. Line two 32 x 28 cm biscuit trays with baking paper.

1 Combine butter, syrup and sugar in a small pan. Stir over low heat until butter melts and sugar dissolves; remove from heat. Add sifted flour and ginger. With wooden spoon, stir until well combined; do not over-beat.

2 Drop 1 level teaspoon of mixture at a time onto prepared trays, about 12 cm apart. (Prepare only three or four biscuits at a time.) Spread mixture into 8 cm rounds. Bake for 6 minutes or until rounds are lacy and bubbling.

3 Leave biscuits on trays for 30 seconds. Remove one from the tray and roll it into a tight tube while it is still hot; leave to cool. Working quickly, repeat the process with remaining biscuits. Dip ends into melted chocolate and place on a foil-covered tray to set. Sprinkle lightly with icing sugar, if desired.

COOK'S FILE

Storage time: Store Brandy Snaps in an airtight container for up to 2 days, or freeze for up to 1 month without dipping in chocolate.

Variation: Roll Brandy Snaps into wider tubes and pipe whipped cream into the middle, if desired. The handle of a wooden spoon is ideal for rolling the biscuits around.

1

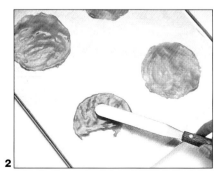

2

3

CHOCOLATE CLUSTERS

Preparation time: 25 minutes
Total cooking time: 3 minutes
Makes about 40

125 g dark choc melts
125 g white choc melts
125 g dried mixed fruit
125 g glacé ginger

➤ PLACE DARK and white choc melts separately into heatproof bowls.
1 Place each bowl over a pan of simmering water and stir gently until melted and smooth. Cool slightly.
2 Stir mixed fruit into dark chocolate. Chop glacé ginger and combine with white chocolate.
3 Spoon mixtures into small paper confectionery cups, leave to set at room temperature.

Storage time: Chocolate Clusters will keep for up to 4 weeks if stored in an airtight container in a cool, dark place.
Hint: Use any single dried fruit, such as raisins or sultanas, instead of mixed fruit, if you prefer. Toasted chopped nuts—pecans, almonds, macadamia or brazil nuts— may also be used instead of fruit.

BAKLAVA FINGERS

Preparation time: 30 minutes
Total cooking time: 20 minutes
Makes 24

Filling
3/4 cup finely chopped walnuts
1 tablespoon brown sugar
1 teaspoon cinnamon
20 g butter, melted

8 sheets filo pastry
50 g butter, melted

Syrup
1 cup sugar
1/2 cup water
2 tablespoons honey
2 teaspoons orange flower
    water, optional

➤ PREHEAT OVEN to moderately hot 210°C. Brush a flat oven tray with oil or melted butter.
1 To make Filling: Place the walnuts, sugar, cinnamon and butter in a small bowl and stir until combined.
2 Working with one at a time, lay a sheet of filo pastry on the work bench. Brush the pastry with melted butter and fold it in half. Cut sheet into 3 strips and place a heaped teaspoon of filling close to the front edge of the pastry. Roll up, tucking in the edges. Place on prepared tray and brush with melted butter.
3 Repeat with remaining pastry sheets. Bake for 15 minutes until fingers are golden brown. Transfer to a wire rack and spoon syrup over the pastries while both the pastries and syrup are still warm.
4 To make Syrup: Combine sugar, water and honey in a small pan. Stir over low heat without boiling until sugar has completely dissolved. Bring to boil, reduce heat and simmer for 5 minutes. Remove from heat and add orange flower water, if desired.

COOK'S FILE

Storage time: Store in an airtight container for up to 2 days.
Note: Baklava Fingers are characteristically very sweet. They are best served with small cups of very strong black coffee.

PECAN-MAPLE SHORTBREADS

Preparation time: 20 minutes
Total cooking time: 20 minutes
Makes about 35

1 cup plain flour
1/2 cup (65 g) ground
    pecans
2 tablespoons icing sugar
90 g butter, chopped

2 tablespoons maple syrup
50 g white choc melts, melted

➤ PREHEAT OVEN to moderate 180°C. Line baking tray with paper.
1 Process flour, nuts, sugar and butter in food processor, using pulse action, 1 minute, until mixture comes together.
2 Turn onto lightly floured surface, press together to form smooth dough. Roll out on a sheet of baking paper to a thickness of 7 mm. Using a 4 cm heart-shaped cutter, cut out shapes

3 Transfer to tray, bake 10 minutes; remove from oven. Brush each shortbread generously with maple syrup, bake another 10 minutes. Transfer biscuits to a wire rack to cool. Spoon white chocolate into small paper piping bag and pipe an outline around edge of biscuits.

COOK'S FILE

Storage time: Pecan-Maple Shortbreads will keep for up to 4 days in an airtight container.

MIXED NUT BISCOTTI

Preparation time: 30 minutes
Total cooking time: 45 minutes
Makes about 50

25 g almonds
25 g hazelnuts
75 g unsalted pistachios
3 egg whites
1/2 cup caster sugar
3/4 cup plain flour

► PREHEAT OVEN to moderate 180°C. Brush a 26 x 8 x 4.5 cm bar tin with oil or melted butter, line base and sides with baking paper.

1 Spread the almonds, hazelnuts and pistachios onto a flat baking tray and place in the oven for 2–3 minutes, until nuts are just toasted; cool. Place the egg whites in a small, clean, dry mixing bowl. Using electric beaters, beat egg whites until stiff peaks form. Add the sugar gradually, beating constantly until the mixture is thick and glossy and all the sugar has dissolved.

2 Transfer mixture to a large mixing bowl. Add sifted flour and nuts. Using a metal spoon, gently fold ingredients together until combined. Spread into prepared tin and smooth the surface. Bake for 25 minutes; remove from oven and cool completely in tin.

3 Preheat the oven to moderately slow 160°C. Using a sharp, serrated knife, cut the baked loaf into 5 mm slices. Spread slices onto oven trays and bake for about 15 minutes, turning once halfway through cooking, until the slices are lightly golden and crisp. Serve Mixed Nut Biscotti to dip into coffee, or with a sweet dessert wine.

COOK'S FILE

Storage time: Mixed Nut Biscotti will keep for up to a week in an airtight container.

Variation: Use any combination of nuts, or a single variety, to the weight of 125 g.

CHOC-DIPPED MACAROONS

Preparation time: 25 minutes
Total cooking time: 15 minutes
Makes about 24

1 egg white
1/3 cup caster sugar
2 teaspoons cornflour
1 cup dessicated coconut
65 g dark compound
    chocolate

► PREHEAT OVEN to moderately slow 160°C. Line a biscuit tray with baking paper.

1 Place the egg white in a small, dry mixing bowl. Using electric beaters, beat until firm peaks form. Add the sugar gradually, beating constantly until the mixture is thick and glossy and all the sugar has dissolved. Add the cornflour and beat until ingredients are just combined.

2 Add the coconut to the egg white mixture. Using a metal spoon, stir until just combined. Roll heaped teaspoons of the mixture into balls and place on the prepared tray. Bake for 15–20 minutes until macaroons are

lightly golden. Remove from the oven and leave to cool on the tray.

3 Place the chocolate in a small bowl over a pan of barely simmering water. When the chocolate is beginning to soften, stir until it is smooth. Dip the tops of the macaroons into the melted chocolate and allow the excess to drain. Place the macaroons on a foil-lined tray and leave to set.

COOK'S FILE

Storage time: Store in an airtight container for up to a day.

Hint: These make a delicious accompaniment for a soft, creamy dessert.

*Mixed Nut Biscotti (top)
and Choc-Dipped Macaroons*

CHOC PRALINE TRIANGLES

Preparation time: 40 minutes
Total cooking time: 3 minutes
Makes 36

½ cup slivered almonds
½ cup caster sugar
150 g dark chocolate, chopped
40 g butter
¼ cup cream
½ cup blanched almonds,
   toasted
200 g dark compound chocolate,
   melted

➤ LINE A flat baking tray with aluminium foil, brush lightly with oil. Line a 20 x 10 cm loaf tin with foil.

1 Combine almonds and sugar in a small pan; place over low heat. Watch carefully, without stirring, until the sugar is melted and golden, about 3–5 minutes. (Tilt pan slightly to dissolve sugar.) Pour onto tray, leave until set and completely cold. Break into chunks, place in plastic bag and crush with rolling pin, or process in food processor until crumbly.

2 Place chopped chocolate in a medium mixing bowl. Combine butter and cream in a small pan; stir over a low heat until butter melts. Bring to boil, remove from heat. Pour hot cream mixture over chocolate. With wooden spoon, stir until chocolate has melted and is smooth. Cool slightly and stir in crushed praline.

3 Spread mixture into prepared tin, smooth surface. Tap gently on bench to level if necessary. Cover with plastic wrap, refrigerate 1 hour or until set. Lift from tin, peel away foil; cut into 36 small triangles.

4 Line a flat tray with foil. Press a whole toasted almond onto each triangle. Using two forks, dip triangles one at a time into chocolate to coat. Lift out, drain off excess chocolate and place onto prepared tray. Leave to set. Pipe with white chocolate to decorate, if desired.

COOK'S FILE

Storage time: Triangles may be stored for up to 1 week in an airtight container in a cool, dark place; refrigerate in warm weather.

SUGAR AND SPICE PALMIERS

Preparation time: 20 minutes
Total cooking time: 20 minutes
Makes 32

1 sheet frozen butter puff
   pastry
2 tablespoons raw sugar
1 teaspoon mixed spice
1 teaspoon ground cinnamon
40 g butter, melted

➤ PREHEAT OVEN to hot 210°C. Brush 2 flat oven trays with melted butter or oil, line with baking paper.
1 Thaw pastry sheet as directed on packet. Combine sugar and spices in small bowl. Cut sheet of pastry in half. Brush pastry sheet with melted butter. Sprinkle generously with sugar mixture, reserving 2 teaspoons.
2 Fold the long edges of pastry inwards, then fold again so that edges almost meet in the centre. Fold once more, place the pastry on a tray and refrigerate for 15 minutes. Using a

small, sharp knife, cut into 32 slices.
3 Arrange palmiers cut-side up onto prepared tray, brush with butter and sprinkle lightly with reserved sugar mixture. Bake for 20 minutes, until golden. Cool palmiers on a wire rack. Dust lightly with icing sugar before serving.

COOK'S FILE

Storage time: Store for up to a day in an airtight container. Palmiers may be re-crisped in a moderate oven for 5 minutes before being served.

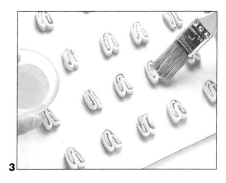

CITRUS ALMOND BISCUITS

Preparation time: 15 minutes +
  20 minutes refrigeration
Total cooking time: 12–15 minutes
Makes 30

60 g butter
1/2 teaspoon grated orange rind
1/2 teaspoon grated lime rind
1/4 cup caster sugar
1/2 cup plain flour
2 tablespoons ground almonds
1 egg white

1 cup flaked almonds, crushed
icing sugar

➤ LINE AN oven tray with baking paper. Preheat the oven to moderate 180°C.

1 Place the butter, orange rind, lime rind and sugar in a small mixing bowl. Using electric beaters, beat until light and creamy.

2 Add the flour and ground almonds and mix with a flat-bladed knife to a soft dough. Press mixture with hands until it comes together.

3 Roll teaspoonsful of the mixture into 2 cm-long logs. Refrigerate for 20 minutes or until mixture is firm. Lightly whisk the egg white with a fork. Lightly crush the flaked almonds with your hands. Place in small bowl. Dip each log into egg white, roll in almonds then place on the prepared tray. Bake in a preheated oven for 12–15 minutes or until lightly golden. Dust with sifted icing sugar while still warm. Allow to cool on tray.

COOK'S FILE

Storage time: Store in airtight container for up to 3 weeks.
Variation: Use lemon rind instead of orange or lime rind if you prefer.

TWO-TONE BISCUITS

Preparation time: 20 minutes +
  20 minutes refrigeration
Total cooking time: 10–12 minutes
Makes about 40

125 g butter
2/3 cup icing sugar
1 egg
1 1/2 cups plain flour
1 tablespoon cornflour
2 tablespoons cocoa powder
50 g dark cooking chocolate,
  melted

➤ PREHEAT OVEN to moderate 180°C. Line two oven trays with baking paper.

1 Beat the butter and icing sugar until light and creamy. Add egg, beat until smooth. Add plain flour and cornflour and mix with a flat-bladed knife until combined.

2 Divide the mixture evenly between 2 bowls. Add the cocoa and melted chocolate to one portion and mix until combined. Wrap the dough portions separately in plastic wrap and refrigerate for 20 minutes or until dough is firm.

3 Roll dough portions separately between sheets of baking paper to a thickness of 4 mm. Use two sizes of biscuit-cutter of the same shape. Cut large shapes from each sheet of dough. Then take the smaller cutter and cut a shape from inside the larger dough shape; swap inner shapes and assemble to make two-tone biscuits. Place biscuits on prepared trays and bake for 10–12 minutes or until just golden. Cool on tray.

COOK'S FILE

Storage time: These biscuits may be stored in an airtight container for up to 4 days.

CHOC-COFFEE CUPS

Preparation time: 35 minutes
Total cooking time: 3 minutes
Makes 20

125 g dark chocolate melts
20 foil confectionery cases
50 g white chocolate, chopped
1 tablespoon cream
1 tablespoon Tia Maria, optional
20 coffee beans
25 g white chocolate melts,
    melted

➤ PLACE DARK chocolate melts in a small heatproof bowl. Stand bowl over a pan of simmering water, stir until chocolate has melted and is smooth. Cool slightly.

1 Working on one at a time, pour a teaspoon of chocolate into each confectionery case. Use a small paintbrush to coat the inside with chocolate, making sure chocolate is thick and there are no gaps. Turn cases upside down onto a wire rack until chocolate coating is firm. Set remaining chocolate aside.

2 Combine white chocolate, cream and Tia Maria in a small heatproof bowl. Stir over a pan of simmering water until melted and smooth. Cool slightly, spoon into chocolate cases. Place a coffee bean into each cup.

3 Reheat the remaining dark chocolate until melted. Spoon a little dark chocolate over the white chocolate to cover, tap cup gently until surface is level. Spoon melted white chocolate melts into a small paper piping bag, pipe a "C" onto each cup. Leave to set.

COOK'S FILE

Storage time: Cups will keep for up to 2 weeks in an airtight container in a cool, dark place. Refrigerate in warmer weather.
Note: The coffee beans may be omitted if you prefer a milder flavour. If you are using them, choose good quality beans.

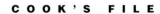

PINE NUT TARTS

Preparation time: 25 minutes
Total cooking time: 15 minutes
Makes 24

1/2 cup plain flour
60 g butter, chopped
1/4 cup pine nuts
20 g butter, melted
1/2 cup golden syrup
2 tablespoons brown sugar

➤ PREHEAT THE OVEN to moderate 180°C. Brush 2 x 12-hole mini muffin tins with melted butter.

1 Place flour and butter in food processor. Using pulse action, press button for 20–30 seconds until mixture comes together. Turn onto a lightly floured surface, press together until smooth.

2 Roll out to a thickness of 3 mm. Cut out rounds with a 5 cm fluted scone cutter. Lift gently with a flat-bladed knife and line each muffin hole with pastry. Spread pine nuts onto a flat oven tray and place in oven for 1–2 minutes, until just golden. Remove from tray and cool; divide nuts between pastry cases.

3 Combine the butter, syrup and sugar in a jug and whisk with a fork. Pour over the pine nuts. Bake for 15 minutes, until golden. Cool tarts in trays for 5 minutes before lifting out onto a wire rack to cool completely. Dust with icing sugar before serving, if desired.

COOK'S FILE

Storage time: Tarts may be made up to 8 hours in advance. Store in an airtight container.
Variation: Use chopped nuts such as walnuts or pecans instead of the pine nuts, if you prefer.

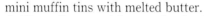

Choc-Coffee Cups (top)
and Pine Nut Tarts

Liqueurs and After-dinner Coffees

CUMQUAT LIQUEUR

Wash and dry 500 g cumquats, then pierce each with a fine skewer. Place cumquats in a large jar, layering with 2 cups of caster sugar. Pour in 1 litre of brandy, gin or vodka; seal and leave in a cool, dark place for at least a month, turning jar regularly. To serve, place one cumquat in each glass and pour liqueur over it. Makes 1 litre of liqueur.

SPICY COFFEE

Make a pot of strong black coffee (enough to make 4 cups) and add 1 teaspoon of cinnamon. Pour coffee into cups and add some Kahlua to taste. Top coffee with whipped cream and decorate with shreds of orange rind. Serves 4.

Clockwise from below: Coffee Liqueur; Whisky Cream; Spicy Coffee; Cumquat Liqueur, Vienna Coffee, Irish Coffee

IRISH COFFEE

Make a pot of strong black coffee and pour into tall—preferably glass—mugs. Add sugar and Irish whiskey to taste, then pour thick cream slowly over the back of a spoon onto the coffee to create a 5 mm-thick layer. Serve immediately. Substitute dark rum for the whiskey to make Jamaican coffee.

COFFEE LIQUEUR

In a large jug, whisk together 1 cup sugar, 3 tablespoons instant coffee powder, 1 cup each of rum and boiling water, and 3 teaspoons of vanilla essence. Pour into a sterilised bottle, seal and store in a cool, dark place for two weeks to allow flavours to develop. Makes about 2½ cups.

WHISKY CREAM

Combine 1 cup cream, 1½ cups evaporated milk, ½ cup condensed milk and 2 tablespoons drinking chocolate in large jug. Slowly stir in 1 cup Scotch whisky; transfer to a sterilised bottle. Store in the refrigerator for up to two weeks. Return to room temperature to serve. Makes 1 litre.

VIENNA COFFEE

Make cups of milky coffee, stir in some grated milk chocolate. Top with a generous dollop of whipped cream and sprinkle with extra grated chocolate. Serve immediately.

CHOCOLATE-ALMOND TARTS

Preparation time: 40 minutes
Total cooking time: 20 minutes
Makes 18

1 cup plain flour
pinch salt
60 g butter, chopped
1 tablespoon icing sugar
1 tablespoon lemon juice

Filling
1 egg
1/3 cup caster sugar
2 tablespoons cocoa
1/2 cup ground almonds
3 tablespoons cream
1/4 cup apricot jam
18 blanched almonds

➤ PREHEAT OVEN to moderate 180°C. Brush two shallow patty cake tins with melted butter or oil.

1 Process flour, salt, butter and icing sugar in food processor, using pulse action, 10 seconds or until fine crumbs form. Add juice, process until mixture forms a ball. Roll between sheets of waxed paper to 6 mm thickness. Cut into 7-cm rounds with fluted cutter. Place in tins, refrigerate 20 minutes.

2 To make Filling: Using electric beaters, beat egg and sugar until thick and pale. Sift cocoa on top. With flat-bladed knife, stir in almonds and cream.

3 Place a dab of jam in centre of each tart. Spoon filling into tarts, place an almond in centre. Bake 15 minutes or until puffed and set on top. Leave in tins 5 minutes then cool on wire racks. Dust with icing sugar if desired.

COOK'S FILE

Storage time: Tarts may be made up to 1 hour in advance.

INDEX

USEFUL INFORMATION

All our recipes are thoroughly tested in the Family Circle® Test Kitchen. Standard metric measuring cups and spoons approved by Standards Australia are used in the development of our recipes. All cup and spoon measurements are level. We have used 60 g eggs in all recipes. Sizes of cans vary from manufacturer to manufacturer and between countries—use the can size closest to the one suggested in the recipes.

Conversion Guide

1 cup = 250 ml (8 fl oz)
1 teaspoon = 5 ml
1 Australian tablespoon = 20 ml (4 teaspoons)
1 UK/US tablespoon = 15 ml (3 teaspoons)

Dry Measures	Liquid Measures	Linear Measures
30 g = 1 oz	30 ml = 1 fl oz	6 mm = $1/4$ inch
250 g = 8 oz	125 ml = 4 fl oz	1 cm = $1/2$ inch
500 g = 1 lb	250 ml = 8 fl oz	2.5 cm = 1 inch

Cup Conversions—Dry Ingredients

1 cup coconut, desiccated	= 90 g (3 oz)
1 cup coconut, shredded	= 50 g (12/3 oz)
1 cup dates, chopped	= 155 g (5 oz)
1 cup flour, plain, or self-raising	= 125 g (4 oz)
1 cup flour, wholemeal	= 125 g (4oz)
1 cup nuts, chopped	= 125 g (4 oz)
1 cup raisins	= 170 g (51/2 oz)
1 cup sugar, granulated	= 170 g (51/2 oz)
1 cup sugar, caster	= 220 g (7 oz)
1 cup sugar, icing	= 170 g (51/2 oz)
1 cup sultanas	= 170 g (51/2 oz)

Oven Temperatures

Electric	°C	°F
Very slow	120	250
Slow	150	300
Mod slow	160	325
Moderate	180	350
Mod hot	210	425
Hot	240	475
Very hot	260	525
Gas	°C	°F
Very slow	120	250
Slow	150	300
Mod slow	160	325
Moderate	180	350
Mod hot	190	375
Hot	200	400
Very hot	230	450

International Glossary

biscuit	cookie
caster sugar	superfine sugar
choc bits	chocolate chips
cornflour	cornstarch
golden syrup	light corn syrup
icing sugar	confectioners' sugar
thickened cream	double cream

Published by Murdoch Books®, a division of Murdoch Magazines Pty Limited, 213 Miller Street, North Sydney NSW 2060.

Murdoch Books® Associate Food Editors: Kerrie Ray, Tracy Rutherford. **Family Circle® Food Editor:** Jo Anne Calabria. **Recipe Development:** Beverly Sutherland Smith, Tracey Port, Jo Richardson, Wendy Brodhurst, Tracy Rutherford. **Home Economists:** Wendy Goggin, Wendy Brodhurst. **Photographer:** Joe Filshie. **Step-by-step Photographer:** Reg Morrison. **Editor:** Deirdre Blayney. **Designer:** Wing Ping Tong. **Food Stylist:** Rosemary De Santis. **Food Stylist's Assistant:** Tracey Port.

Publisher: Anne Wilson. **Publishing Manager:** Catie Ziller. **Production Coordinator:** Liz Fitzgerald. **Managing Editor:** Susan Tomnay. **Studio Manager:** Norman Baptista. **International Manager:** Mark Newman. **Marketing Manager:** Mark Smith. **National Sales Manager:** Keith Watson. **Key Accounts Sales Manager:** Kim Deacon. **Photo Librarian:** Dianne Bedford.

National Library of Australia Cataloguing-in-Publication Data. Desserts and after dinner treats. Includes index. ISBN 0 86411 424 9 1. Desserts 2. Confectionery. I. Title. 641.89. Printed by Prestige Litho, Queensland.